Wedding Knits

Wedding Knits

Handknit Gifts for Every Member of the Wedding Party

A Lark Production

POTTER
CRAFT

SUSS COUSINS

PHOTOGRAPHY BY SUZUKI K

Copyright © 2007 by Suss Cousins

Photographs © 2007 by Kaori Suzuki, aka Suzuki K

Published in the United States by Potter Craft, an imprint of the Crown
Publishing Group, a division of Random House, Inc., New York.
www.crownpublishing.com
www.pottercraft.com

POTTER CRAFT and CLARKSON N. POTTER are trademarks, and POTTER
and colophon are registered trademarks of Random House, Inc.

Library of Congress Cataloging-in-Publication Data
Cousins, Suss.
   Wedding knits / handknit gifts for every member of the wedding party / Suss Cousins;
photographs by Suzuki K.
         p. cm.
   Includes index.
1. Knitting—Patterns.   2. Wedding costume.   I. Title.
TT820.C856 2007
746.43'2041—dc22   2006014140

ISBN-13: 978-0-307-34640-7
ISBN-10: 0-307-34640-4

Printed in Singapore

Design by Blue Cup Design, Inc.

10 9 8 7 6 5 4 3 2 1

First Edition

To my husband, Brian

contents

introduction

2

for the
bride

3

for the wedding night and
honeymoon

Introduction

When I was growing up in Sweden, I used to fantasize about weddings, just like millions of other young girls all around the world. I loved the wedding in an old Ingmar Bergman film, where the bride is dancing on a huge grassy lawn in a classic white Swedish dress, with flowers both in her hair and spilling all over the ground. I imagined the new couple feasting on sweet lobster and homemade bread and drinking champagne. Designing the patterns for this book is like that vision made real. I got to recreate a fantasy wedding in my mind and then in my studio, and finally in the gorgeous photo shoot we had, complete with lobster and champagne! ✳ Of course, the first project I came up with had to be a stunning wedding dress. It set the theme for all the other wedding designs: lots of different stitches and textures, delicate yarn, many small beautiful details, very light and, best of all, comfortable! I wanted my fantasy bride to be able to dance all night if she wanted to. ✳ Once I had the dress set, I knew the bride would need equally elegant accessories. But I wanted to give her a choice, so I offer both a short veil and a long veil, two deluxe purses, and a pair of special wraps. ✳ My friends and family are very important in my life, so I had to include projects for the bride's attendants and relatives as well. I wanted to give bridesmaids a chance to shine, either by offering personal, one-of-a-kind gifts the bride can knit for them or by providing patterns for them to knit their own unique outfits and wedding presents. Grandmother, mother, and friends can knit their love right into the projects they make—which is much more intimate than buying everything for the wedding. ✳ My strongest memory of my own grandmother is of her knitting, and if she had been able to knit my wedding dress, it would have been incredible and would have brought us even closer together. She never had the chance because she passed away when I was 15. When I did get married, the wedding was very simple, just how I wanted it to be. My husband and I were married at City Hall in Manhattan in late January. I wore a salmon skirt and a white blouse that I had bought off the rack—at least it was a knit!—while my husband wore a white suit with a salmon-colored tie. Although it wasn't a classic outdoor wedding on the grass, it was so beautiful, and we had an unforgettable celebration. A very close friend made our day special by holding a wonderful dinner party in his restaurant for all of our friends. Months later we spent our honeymoon camping on a pretty beach in Florida. It couldn't have been more romantic! ✳ If we had had a traditional wedding, I would have gotten married outside on the grass in a big garden, surrounded by trees and sky and fresh air. My favorite weddings have all been outdoors. Two of my friends were married on a white sandy beach facing the ocean. My brother was married poolside in sunny Los Angeles, while another friend was married in a casual barefoot ceremony on a sparkling clear afternoon under the blue sky on top of a hill in upstate New York. I love a gorgeous setting like that, the early spring air smelling delicious, and everything a pale chartreuse green. The whole event can be very simple, yet lush. ✳ Beautiful, romantic, unique, and elegant, the patterns I designed for this book work for weddings in any season. Hand-knitted wedding essentials—like a ring pillow, the must-have something-blue garter, and sexy lingerie for the wedding night—are timeless yet original, just as you want to be. I used exquisite textured stitches such as seed stitch, open lace stitch, tiny cables, and small needles to create delicate knits. I've used luxurious yarns that are soft and feminine, with a very fine hand: 100% silk, fine mohair, angora, baby alpaca, mercerized cotton, and fabulous novelty blends. The colors are a muted palette of ivories, pale pinks, and greens, with names like Pearl, Rose Blush, Purity, and Silver Birch. I introduce shimmer in the form of Austrian crystals, rose quartz, silver and gold threads, mother of pearl, satin ribbons, and chiffon bows. Every project sparkles, shines, or stands out, making it extra special for the world of weddings. I was careful to include easy projects that knit up in no time as well as a more challenging, intricate, inspirational pattern for a hand-knitted wedding gown. So whether you're a beginning knitter or a very advanced knitter, you can find patterns to suit every step of your walk down the aisle. ☀ The first section is **For the Bridal Party.** A Luxe Bridesmaid Purse, Belted Tunic Dress, Bridesmaid Wrap, Mother-of-the-Bride Handkerchief, and Rosebud Hair Clip are just some of the fun items you can start knitting the minute there's a wedding on your calendar. ☀ In the next part, **For the Bride,** you get to dream about how you'd look in the Ultimate Wedding Dress, with its silk, alpaca, pearls, and crystals. Or choose from two different veils, one classic one made special with ivory ribbon, roses, and iridescent sequins, the other knit in gorgeous cloverleaf lace. Finish off your bridal outfit with Fingerless Long Gloves and a Wedding Wrap woven with champagne silk ribbon. ☀ Finally, you get to knit for your wedding night in **For the Wedding Night and Honeymoon.** Projects like the sexy Wedding Night Robe and sweet Angora Camisole and Shorts Set live up to this once-in-a-lifetime event. The softest yarn, the palest flower embroidery, crocheted butterflies, Austrian crystal, and organza all contribute to creating that special mood for the wedding night and beyond, during your honeymoon. ☀ If you are getting married or are part of a bridal party, no doubt the wedding has become a large part of your life. If you also happen to be a knitter, what could be more natural than knitting your way through the months of planning and preparation leading up to the big day? This is a great opportunity to apply your passion for knitting to an important occasion. Weddings usually take a long time to organize, so you can pick several projects and make the wedding a special handcrafted experience. Without spending a fortune, you can create a unique-looking wedding, which is what every bride I've ever met wants. ☀ Whether you pick the yarn together with the bride or make your gift a surprise, you'll find knitting the projects in this book fulfilling. I know from personal experience. Although I've been married for twenty-two years, I am surrounded by friends and relatives getting married. I love to knit for every one of them, from a veil to a shawl to the ring pillows. I'm so happy to share these patterns, inspired by the special people in my life for you to share with the special people in your life.

1

All the projects in this section are designed for members of the wedding party to wear, from head (Rosebud Hair Clip) to shoulders (Maid-of-Honor Shrug) to hands (Mother-of-the-Bride Handkerchief). Either the bridesmaids can make them or the knitting bride could surprise her bridesmaids. ✳ My favorite project for the bridal party is the Belted Tunic Dress—it's impossible for any bridesmaid not to look even better in this outfit. You knit in a slub cotton yarn on circular needles in three easy pieces. Topped with the mint-colored Bridesmaid Wrap, it makes for a beautiful, unified look during the ceremony and reception. ✳ Between the Knitted Headband and the Rosebud Hair Clip, I have your bridesmaids' heads covered. The headband is the fastest pattern to knit in the book. Finished with pearls and fringe, it defintely says "wedding." ✳ You brides know how hard it is to come up with original, affordable gifts for your bridesmaids. The personalized Charmed Bracelet and the Luxe Bridesmaid Purse will come to your rescue. You make the bracelet in seed stitch out of silvery metallic yarn while the purse is a chunky, ribbed camel knit with a retro closure made from a vintage pin.

13

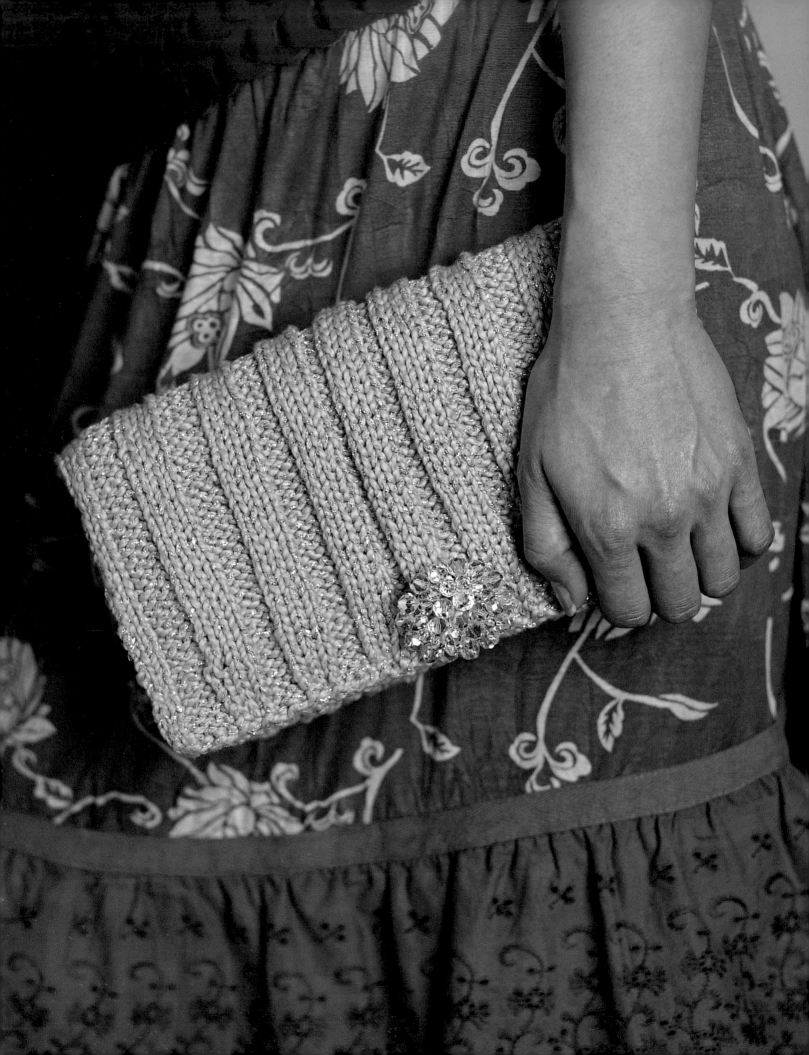

1. luxe bridesmaid purse

I love to collect vintage jewelry, especially pins, from the 1930s and 1940s. I go to flea markets all the time and sometimes find great pieces. After buying this beautiful brooch, I had the idea of making a very simply shaped clutch in a rib stitch—like something out of a Greta Garbo movie. Together with golden yarn, the brooch's sparkle makes this purse shine. After the wedding is over, you can use it for any special evening event. The color is neutral enough to go with everything.

luxe bridesmaid purse

Experience Level:
Intermediate

Finished Measurements:
Outside cover: 10½" wide × 12" long/26.5 cm × 30.5 cm
Inside panel: 10½" wide × 11" long/26.5 cm × 28 cm

Yarns:
A: 2 skeins Suss Cotton (100% cotton; 2.5 ounces/71 grams; 118 yards/109 meters),
color Honey
B: 1 ball Suss Lurex (65% nylon/35% metallic; 1 ounce/29 grams; 225 yards/208 meters,
color Gold

Notions:
1   pair size 8 (5 mm) needles
1   stitch holder
large tapestry needle
sewing needle and thread in complementary color
sewing pins
1   invisible zipper, 10"/25 cm long
1   piece sewing interfacing, 10½" × 12"/ 26.5 cm × 30.5 cm
(available at most fabric and craft stores)
1   piece of honey-colored linen, 11½" × 13"/29 cm × 33 cm
1   vintage sparkly brooch

Gauge:
22 stitches and 24 rows = 4"/10 cm in three-by-three rib stitch with one strand yarn A
and one strand yarn B held together

PURSE:
To make the outside cover, cast on 57 stitches with one strand of yarn A and one strand of yarn B held together. Work in a three-by-three rib stitch (knit 3 stitches, purl 3 stitches, repeat until you have 3 stitches remaining, knit 3 stitches) until the piece measures 12"/30.5 cm, or approximately 72 rows.

Bind off in rib pattern.

To make the inside panel, cast on 57 stitches with one strand of yarn A and one strand of yarn B held together. Work in a three-by-three rib stitch until the piece measures 5½"/14 cm, or approximately 33 rows.

To make zipper slit, work 6 stitches in rib pattern, bind off 45 stitches, and place remaining 6 stitches on a stitch holder. Cut yarn leaving a tail approximately 12"/30.5 cm. Join yarn and work the 6 stitches on the needle in rib pattern for two rows. At the end of the second row, cast on 45 stitches using the single cast-on method as follows: make a loop with the working yarn and slip it over your left thumb with the end attached to the right needle closest to your fingers. Hold the two ends of yarn in the palm of your left hand with your fingers. Insert the needle under the end attached to the ball of yarn (which should be the end closest to your wrist) and pull upwards forming a small loop on the needle. Pull the loop tight. Repeat until you have added 45 stitches.

Pick up and work the 6 stitches on stitch holder in rib pattern. Work the first stitch using both the working yarn *and* the 12"/30.5 cm tail (this will help anchor the joining of these two sections). On the next row, make sure you work this stitch as a single stitch only. There will be one less row in this section than in the corresponding section on the other end of the zipper slit.

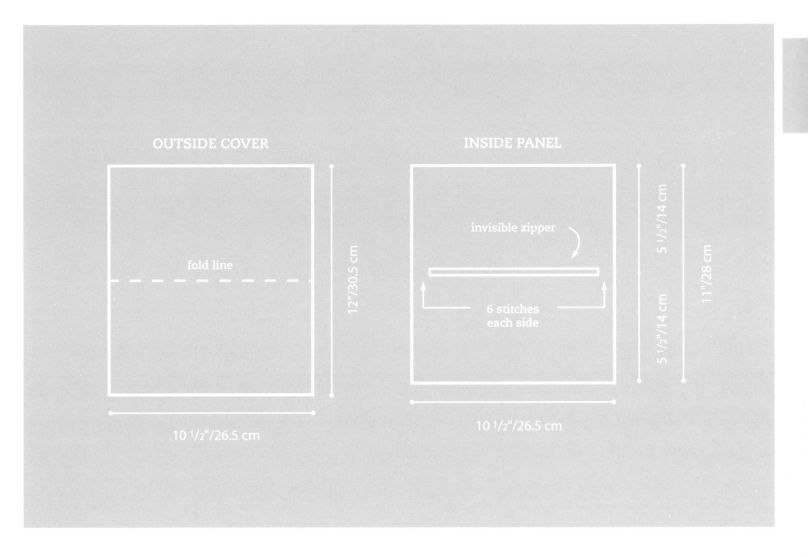

OUTSIDE COVER

fold line

12"/30.5 cm

10 ½"/26.5 cm

INSIDE PANEL

invisible zipper

6 stitches each side

5 ½"/14 cm

5 ½"/14 cm

11"/28 cm

10 ½"/26.5 cm

Continue working in the three-by-three rib stitch across all 57 stitches until the inside panel measures 11"/28 cm from cast-on edge.

Bind off in rib pattern.

FINISHING:
Weave in all loose ends with the tapestry needle.

Place the piece of linen on top of the interfacing with the right side facing out. Fold the edges of the linen over the interfacing (approximately ½"/1 cm on all sides) and pin the linen to the interfacing. Pin the linen/interfacing to the wrong side of the outside cover, matching up all the edges. Whipstitch the linen and interfacing to the knitted piece using the sewing needle and thread. Remove the pins as you go.

Center the invisible zipper over the slit in the middle of the inside panel and pin it evenly to the wrong side of

the inside panel on both sides of this slit. The knitted edges should be lined up quite closely to the zipper itself. Test to make sure that the zipper opens and closes easily before sewing, and make any adjustments you need. With the sewing needle and thread, whipstitch the invisible zipper securely to the wrong side of the inside panel. Make sure your stitches are not visible on the other side of the knitted piece.

Place the inside panel and the outside cover with their wrong sides facing each other and pin them together. The outside cover piece is slightly longer than the inside panel to allow the cover more room to fold. Stretch the inside panel piece slightly to fit. With the tapestry needle and one strand of yarn A, seam together all four edges. Fold the purse over to make it a clutch purse.

Pin the vintage brooch on the outside of the purse and you're ready to carry this bag up the aisle or out for a night on the town.

2. knitted headband

Growing up in Sweden, I always wore scarves or bandannas tied around my head to keep the hair out of my face. Lately, I've been wearing a black headband—it makes me feel so productive that I get a lot done. I make headbands like this all the time for a guy friend because his hair is so long! I made this wedding party pattern very feminine with fresh-water pearls and fringe. What's great about all your bridesmaids wearing a headband is that it gives them a unified look, no matter what hairstyle they may have. It is also good for making a bridesmaid with short hair look more dressed up for the wedding. It's easy to make, and the yarn comes in four other colors, if you prefer.

knitted headband

Experience Level:
Beginner

Size:
One size fits all

Finished Measurements:
3" wide × 45" long/7.5 cm × 114 cm

Yarn:
2 skeins Suss Meadow (60% cotton/40% viscose; 1.5ounces/43 grams; 90 yards/83 meters), color Honeydew

Notions:
1   pair size 7 (4.5 mm) needles
     large tapestry needle
4   pink freshwater pearl beads approximately ½"/.5 cm each
     sewing needle and thread in complementary color
1   size G (4 mm) crochet hook

Gauge:
22 stitches and 35 rows = 4"/10 cm in seed stitch

HEADBAND:
Cast on 16 stitches. Work in seed stitch (described below) until piece measures 45"/114 cm long.

To work seed stitch:

Row 1: Knit 1 stitch, purl 1 stitch, repeat until the end of the row.

Row 2: Purl all knit stitches and purl all knit stitches.

Repeat rows 1 and 2.

Bind off in seed stitch.

FINISHING:
Weave in all loose ends with the tapestry needle.

Fold the headband in half to find the center and, with the sewing needle and thread, attach the beads near the center somewhat randomly about 1"/2.5 cm apart from each other (see photograph). Make sure you attach the beads securely by threading the needle through the beads and the headband at least twice before tying off the thread.

To make fringe, cut 20 lengths of yarn approximately 4"/10 cm each. Take one length of yarn and fold it in half, forming a loop. Insert the crochet hook into one of the corners of the narrow edges of the headband and pull the loop of yarn through from the other side of the headband. Then pull the length of yarn through that loop and tighten it to make your first fringe tassel. On each of the narrow edges of the headband, attach 10 fringe tassels placed about ⅓"/.8 cm apart.

Tie the headband around your head with the pearl beads in the front.

3"/7.5 cm

45"/114 cm

3. rosebud hair clip

In my stores, I sell rubber hair bands with little knitted flowers attached. So I adapted that idea to make a hair ornament bridesmaids could wear in the wedding. Using a barrette as the base means that no matter what her hairstyle, each bridesmaid will be able to find a flattering way to wear this piece. The light green yarn that covers the clip looks like leaves and the textured yarn makes sweet roses. Such a small item knits up fast enough that you can make as many as you need in a short time.

rosebud hair clip

Experience Level:
Intermediate

Size:

Fits barrette 5"/13 cm long and ¾"/2 cm wide

Rosebud: approximately 11" long × 1½" wide/28 cm × 4 cm (see diagram)
Barrette cover: 5" long × 1" wide/13 cm × 2.5 cm
Leaf: 3" long × 1" wide/7.5 cm × 2.5 cm

Yarns:

A: 1 skein Suss Charm (70% cotton/30% nylon; 2 ounces/57 grams; 46 yards/42 meters),
color Baby Pink
B: 1 ball Suss Perle Cotton (100% cotton; 2 ounces/57 grams; 256 yards/236 meters),
color Dark Mushroom
C: 1 ball Suss Perle Cotton (100% cotton; 2 ounces/57 grams; 256 yards/236 meters),
color Willow

Notions:

1 pair size 10 (6 mm) needles
1 size B (2.25 mm) crochet hook
tapestry needle
1 barrette, 5"/13 cm long × ¾"/2 cm wide

Gauge:
16 stitches and 16 rows = 4"/10cm in stockinette stitch with yarn A

ROSEBUD:
With yarn A, cast on 44 stitches.

Row 1: Knit all stitches.

Row 2: Purl 2 together, purl all stitches until the last 2, purl 2 together—42 stitches total.

Rows 3 and 5: Knit 1, [knit 2, make 1 stitch, knit 1, make 1 stitch, knit 3, (knit 2 together twice)], repeat until last stitch, knit 1.

Row 4: Purl all stitches.

Row 6: Purl 2 together across the entire row—21 stitches total.

Row 7: [Knit 2 together] 10 times, knit 1—11 stitches total.

Row 8: Purl all stitches.

To make 1 stitch: With the working yarn in back, insert the right needle from front to back underneath the horizontal bar connecting the two stitches in the row below the one you're working. Place that loop on the left needle. Knit *into the front* of that loop (this will cause the loop to twist slightly and prevent a hole from being created).

Cut the yarn, leaving a 12"/30.5 cm tail. Thread tail through the tapestry needle. Insert tapestry needle through the stitches on the knitting needle, pulling each stitch off the knitting needle as you go. Pull the stitches together tightly while twisting the knitted piece in a circle to create the rose. Secure the yarn by looping it around a couple of the stitches on the bottom of the rose but *do not tie off or cut the yarn.*

Make two roses.

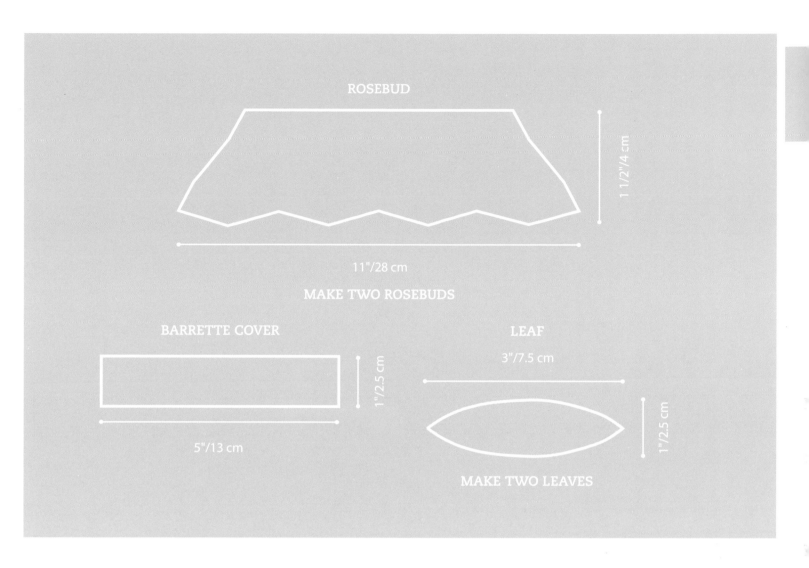

ROSEBUD

1 1/2"/4 cm

11"/28 cm

MAKE TWO ROSEBUDS

BARRETTE COVER

1"/2.5 cm

5"/13 cm

LEAF

3"/7.5 cm

1"/2.5 cm

MAKE TWO LEAVES

Since you will be working with two strands of yarn, begin by dividing the yarn into two balls of equal size.

With the crochet hook and two strands of yarn B, chain 28 stitches.

Work 2 rows of triple crochet and fasten off.

LEAF:
Since you will be working with two strands of yarn, begin by dividing the yarn into two balls of equal size.

With the crochet hook and two strands of yarn C, chain 19 stitches.

Work 1 single crochet stitch, 3 double crochets, 10 triple crochets, 3 double crochets, and 1 single crochet.

Turn, chain 1, and repeat the same crochet pattern on the reverse side of the foundation chain to create the other half of the leaf pattern.

Make two leaves.

FINISHING:
Stretch the barrette cover tightly over the top of the barrette and whipstitch the edges together securely on the underside of the barrette using the tapestry needle and two strands of yarn B.

With the tapestry needle and two strands of yarn B, attach the rosebuds to the top of the barrette securely. Each rosebud should be placed approximately ½"/1cm from the center of the top of the barrette. Attach one leaf under each rosebud with the tapestry needle and yarn B so that an inch or so of leaf is extending beyond the sides of the barrette.

4. belted tunic dress

An elegant, 1940s-inspired piece knit with 100% cotton slub yarn in a seed stitch pattern will stay comfortable during a long wedding day. The dress is a classic shape that's exactly the kind of bridesmaid dress everyone wants: both flattering during the wedding and versatile for using afterward. It looks perfect with high heels and a pearl necklace, plus you can wear it over a silk camisole, with pants or a long skirt, or even over a bikini in the summer.

belted tunic dress

Experience Level:
Advanced

Sizes:
Small (medium, large, extra large)

Finished Measurements:
Chest: 34" (36", 38", 40")/86 (91, 96.5, 101.5) cm
Length: 36" (37", 38", 39")/91 (94, 96.5, 99) cm

Yarn:
9 (9, 10, 10) skeins Suss Twisted (100% slub cotton; 2.5 ounces/71 grams; 108 yards/100 meters), color Nude

Notions:
- 1 pair size 10 (6 mm) circular needles, 24"/61 cm long
- 1 knitting row counter
- 4 stitch markers
- 1 pair size 7 (4.5 mm) needles
  large tapestry needle
  sewing pins
- 1 size G (4 mm) crochet hook

Gauge:
17 stitches and 24 rows = 4"/10 cm in seed stitch with size 10 needles
24 stitches and 25 rows = 4"/10 cm in one-by-one rib stitch with size 7 needles

BACK:

Cast on 64 (68, 72, 76) stitches with size 10 needles. Work in seed stitch (see page 20) for one row.

Cast on 4 stitches at the beginning of every row for 8 rows—96 (100, 104, 108) stitches, 9 rows total. You may wish to use a row counter for this project. Cast on 5 stitches at the beginning of the next 2 rows—106 (110, 114, 118) stitches, 11 rows total. Work the added stitches in the seed stitch pattern.

Decrease 1 stitch at the beginning and end of every 10 rows 4 (5, 6, 8) times—98 (100, 102, 102) stitches, 41 (51, 61, 81) rows total. Decrease 1 stitch at the beginning and end of every 8 rows 13 (12, 11, 9) times—72 (76, 80, 84) stitches, 145 (147, 149, 153) rows total.

To make cap sleeves, increase 1 stitch at the beginning and end of every 4 rows 10 (12, 13, 14) times—92 (100, 106, 112) stitches, 185 (195, 201, 209) rows total. Increase 1 stitch at the beginning and end of every 2 rows 4 (2, 1, 0) times—100 (104, 108, 112) stitches, 193 (199, 203, 209) rows total.

INCREASES AND DECREASES:

To increase stitches on a knit row: insert the right needle as if you were going to knit, wrap the yarn around the needle, and draw the loop of yarn through but *do not* remove the stitch from the left needle.

Re-insert the right needle into the back of the same stitch, wrap the yarn around the needle and pull it through. Slip the stitch off the left needle.

To increase stitches on a purl row: insert the right needle as if you were going to purl, wrap the yarn around the needle, and draw the loop of yarn through but *do not* remove the stitch from the left needle.

Re-insert the right needle into the back of the same stitch, wrap the yarn around the needle, and pull it through. Slip the stitch off the left needle.

To decrease stitches on a purl row: purl two stitches together at the same time.

To decrease stitches on a knit row: knit two stitches together at the same time.

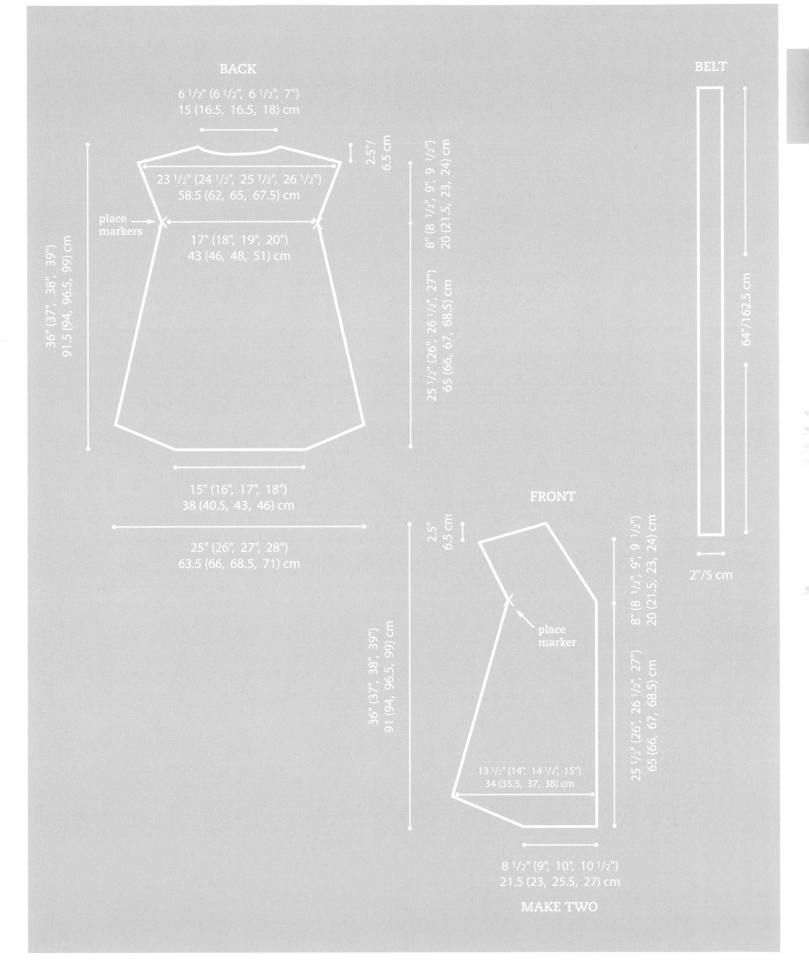

BACK

6 1/2" (6 1/2", 6 1/2", 7")
15 (16.5, 16.5, 18) cm

2.5"/
6.5 cm

23 1/2" (24 1/2", 25 1/2", 26 1/2")
58.5 (62, 65, 67.5) cm

8" (8 1/2", 9", 9 1/2") cm
20 (21.5, 23, 24) cm

place markers

17" (18", 19", 20")
43 (46, 48, 51) cm

25 1/2" (26", 26 1/2", 27")
65 (66, 67, 68.5) cm

36" (37", 38", 39")
91.5 (94, 96.5, 99) cm

15" (16", 17", 18")
38 (40.5, 43, 46) cm

25" (26", 27", 28")
63.5 (66, 68.5, 71) cm

BELT

64"/162.5 cm

2"/5 cm

FRONT

2.5"
6.5 cm

8" (8 1/2", 9", 9 1/2")
20 (21.5, 23, 24) cm

place marker

36" (37", 38", 39") cm
91 (94, 96.5, 99) cm

25 1/2" (26", 26 1/2", 27")
65 (66, 67, 68.5) cm

13 1/2" (14", 14 1/2", 15")
34 (35.5, 37, 38) cm

8 1/2" (9", 10", 10 1/2")
21.5 (23, 25.5, 27) cm

MAKE TWO

Bind off 5 stitches at the beginning of every row 12 (12, 8, 10) times—40 (44, 68, 62) stitches, 205 (211, 211, 219) rows total. Bind off 3 (4, 4, 4) stitches at the beginning of every row 4 (4, 10, 8) times—28 (28, 28, 30) stitches, 209 (215, 221, 227) rows total.

Bind off loosely in seed stitch pattern.

FRONT:

Cast on 36 (38, 42, 44) stitches with size 10 needles. Work in seed stitch for one row. Cast on 4 stitches to the beginning of the next row—40 (42, 46, 48) stitches. Cast on 4 stitches at the beginning of every even-numbered row 3 times—52 (54, 58, 60) stitches, 8 rows total. Cast on 5 stitches to the beginning of the next (even-numbered) row—57 (59, 63, 65) stitches, 10 rows total. Work even one row.

Decrease 1 stitch at the beginning of every 10 rows 4 (5, 6, 8) times—53 (54, 57, 57) stitches, 41 (51, 61, 81) rows total. Until sleeve and neckline shaping, make sure you work all the decreases at the beginning of even-numbered rows. Decrease 1 stitch at the beginning of every 8 rows 13 (12, 11, 9) times—40 (42, 46, 48) stitches, 145 (147, 149, 153) rows total. Place stitch marker at the beginning of the next (wrong-side) row. This stitch marker should be on the same edge of the piece as the decreases.

To shape cap sleeve and neckline, increase 1 stitch at the beginning and decrease 1 stitch at the end of every 4 wrong-side rows 10 (12, 13, 14) times—40 (42, 46, 48) stitches, 185 (195, 201, 209) rows total. Increase 1 stitch at the beginning and decrease 1 stitch at the end of every 2 rows (4 (2, 1, 0) times—40 (42, 46, 48) stitches, 193 (199, 203, 209) rows total.

Bind off 5 stitches at the beginning of every wrong-side row 6 (6, 4, 5) times—10 (12, 26, 23) stitches, 205 (211, 211, 219) rows total. Bind off 3 (4, 4, 4) stitches at the beginning of every wrong-side row 2 (2, 5, 4) times—4 (4, 6, 7) stitches, 209 (215, 221, 227) rows total. Bind off remaining stitches.

Make two. The right and left Front pieces are reversible and identical.

BELT:

Cast on 12 stitches with size 7 needles.

Work in a one-by-one rib stitch (knit 1 stitch, purl 1 stitch, repeat until the end of the row) until Belt measures 64"/162.5 cm, or whatever length you choose.

Bind off.

FINISHING:

Weave in all loose ends with the tapestry needle.

Since the two Front pieces are reversible, place them side by side in a mirrored position to each other. Line up the shoulder seams of each Front piece with the shoulder seams of the Back. Pin together the shoulder seams and, with the tapestry needle and yarn, sew the shoulder seams using backstitch. Pin the side seams together making sure you line up the stitch markers as your guides. Sew the side seams using backstitch, starting at the bottom hem and stopping at the stitch markers.

With the crochet hook, work a single crochet around all the edges of the tunic including the bottom hem, neckline, and sleeves.

To make the Belt loops, use the crochet hook to make two chains approximately 3"/8 cm long and, with the tapestry needle and yarn, attach them securely to the side seams so the top of the loop lies approximately 4"/10 cm below the bottom of the armhole. You may want to try on the garment first and mark where you would like the Belt to be placed.

When you're done with the belt loops, thread the belt through these two loops, tie it around your waist, and you're done!

5. spa tote bag

Fill this oblong tote with beauty products and you'll have the perfect gift for your brides-maids. The braided handle divides the tote into three sections for keeping everything organized. It's very sturdy, yet pretty and feminine in rose quartz with cute leather hearts. Or you could make it for the groom in a dark color and no hearts; a set would make an original wedding gift. The couple could bring them poolside on their honeymoon!

spa tote bag

Experience Level:
Advanced

Finished Measurements of Tote Bag:
14" width × 4" depth × 7" height/36 cm × 10 cm × 18 cm

Yarn:
4 skeins Suss Cotton (100% cotton; 2.5 ounces/71 grams; 118 yards/109 meters), color Rose Blush

Notions:
- 1 pair size 4 (3.5 mm) needles
  large tapestry needle
  sewing pins
- 1 size G (4 mm) crochet hook
  sewing needle and thread in complementary color
- 1 cream aluminum zipper, 14"/35.5 long (available at any fabric store)
- 2 3"/8 cm pink leather hearts (available at www.sussdesign.com)

Gauge:
20 stitches and 30 rows = 4"/10 cm in stockinette stitch

BOTTOM:
Cast on 70 stitches. Work in stockinette stitch (knit all right-side rows and purl all wrong-side rows) until piece measures 4"/10 cm, or 30 rows. Bind off.

SIDE PANELS:
Cast on 70 stitches. Work in stockinette until piece measures 7"/18 cm, or 54 rows. Bind off.

Make two.

INTERIOR PANELS:
Cast on 70 stitches. Work in stockinette until piece measures 6"/15.5 cm, or 46 rows. Bind off.

Make two.

TOP PANELS:
Cast on 70 stitches. Work in stockinette until piece measures 2"/5 cm, or 15 rows. Bind off.

Make two.

END PANELS:
Cast on 20 stitches. Work in stockinette until piece measures 7"/18 cm, or 54 rows. Bind off.

Make two.

FINISHING:
Weave in all loose ends with the tapestry needle.

Fold one of the Side Panels in four to find the center and mark this center with a pin. Pin one of the pink leather hearts to this center on the right side of the Side Panel. With the tapestry needle and yarn, whipstitch the heart to the Side Panel. Repeat for the other Side Panel.

To make the interior pockets, fold one of the Side Panels and one of the Interior Panels in thirds (see diagram) and, on the right side of each, mark these folds with sewing pins. With one of the long (14"/36 cm) edges lined up, place the Interior Panel and the Side Panel together with the wrong sides facing. Pin the two pieces together. With the tapestry needle and yarn, sew the two panels together along the two fold lines marked by the sewing pins using a simple running stitch. To give stability to the interior pockets and alleviate some of the "stockinette roll," work a single crochet across the top edge of the Interior Panel.

Repeat for the other Side and Interior Panels.

Place the two Top Panels with wrong sides facing and whipstitch the two pieces together for ½"/1 cm at the beginning and end of one of the long edges. Pin the zipper into the slit created between the two Top Panels

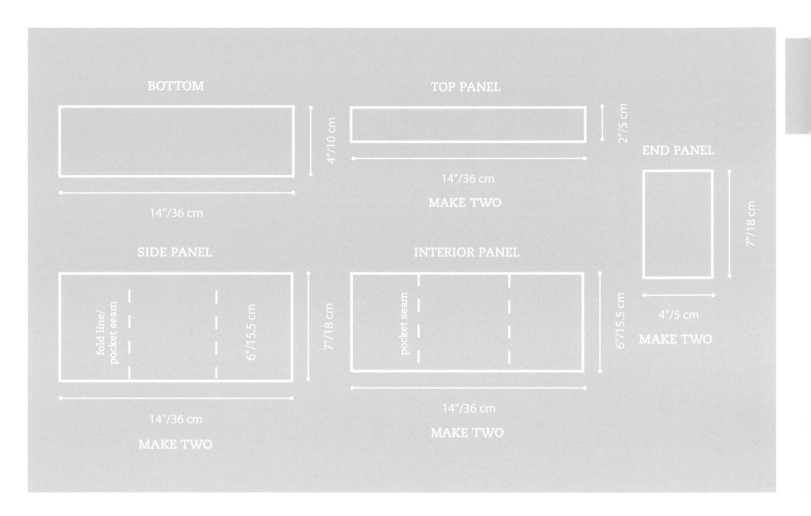

BOTTOM

14"/36 cm

4"/10 cm

TOP PANEL

14"/36 cm

2"/5 cm

MAKE TWO

END PANEL

7"/18 cm

4"/5 cm

MAKE TWO

SIDE PANEL

fold line/
pocket seam

6"/15.5 cm

7"/18 cm

14"/36 cm

MAKE TWO

INTERIOR PANEL

pocket seam

6"/15.5 cm

14"/36 cm

MAKE TWO

with the knitted edges approximately ¼"/0.5 cm from the zipper. Test to make sure that the zipper opens and closes easily before sewing and make any adjustments you need. With the sewing needle and thread, sew the zipper securely to the two Top Panels.

To assemble the bag, pin together the Side Panels to the Bottom with the wrong sides facing. Pin the End Panels to the Bottom and the Side Panels in a similar fashion. With the tapestry needle and yarn, sew the pieces together using backstitch. Work your stitches close to the edges and make sure you use small stitches to ensure that the hem is secure and that the bag is durable. Leave a small 1"/2.5 cm opening in the seam between the Side Panel and the Bottom at one of the fold lines/pocket seams. With the wrong sides facing, pin and sew the Top Panels to the top edges of the Side and End Panels.

To make the handles, cut yarn into 30 strands 3 yards/3 meters long. Wrap a piece of yarn a few times around one end and tie it tightly. Divide the strands into three groups of ten. Braid these three groups together and

secure the end by wrapping a piece of yarn around it and tying it tightly. If you want to make the handles longer, make a longer braid. Cut the strands approximately 50% longer than the total desired length since the braiding process will "shrink" the handle to about ⅔ the original length of the strands. The length I suggest will make handles about 10"/25.5 cm long.

Insert one end of the braid into the 1"/2.5 cm hole in the seam between the Bottom and the Side Panel and attach securely with the tapestry needle and yarn, but do not close the hole.

Pin the braid up the Side Panel of the bag along the line formed by the pocket seam (the braid handle will cover this seam), form a loop for a handle (approximately 10"/25.5 cm), and continue to pin the braid down the other pocket seam and across the Bottom of the bag. Pin the braid to the other Side Panel in a similar fashion to the first and pin the braid across the Bottom of the bag to the starting point. Stitch up both braid ends and close the 1"/2.5 cm hole. Whipstitch the braid to the bag securely.

6. heirloom wedding album

Now that we live in such a digital age, it seems all too easy to forget to make copies of photos for scrapbooks. You might as well not bother taking pictures in the first place! I really miss old-fashioned photograph albums, and a bride deserves an extra luxurious album to remember her special day. Using two slightly different colored yarns creates a soft checkerboard pattern. It's not that hard to make this album for someone getting married, yet it's sure to be appreciated. If you like, enclose a photo or a drawing on the front to personalize it.

heirloom wedding album

Experience Level:
Intermediate

Size:
To fit photo album 10" wide × 9" tall/25 cm × 23 cm

Finished Measurements:
10" wide × 9" tall/25 cm × 23 cm (each panel)

Yarns:
A: 3 skeins Suss Cotton (100% cotton; 2.5 ounces/71 grams; 118 yards/109 meters), color Purity
B: 1 skein Suss Cotton (100% cotton; 2.5 ounces/71 grams; 118 yards/109 meters), color Naturale

Notions:
1   pair size 6 (4 mm) needles
2   stitch holders
     large tapestry needle
1   photo album with ribbon ties, 10" wide × 9"/25 × 23 cm tall with 2½" × 2½"/6.5 cm × 6.5 cm opening for photo (available at art supply stores and most major bookstores), color ivory
1   size G (4 mm) crochet hook
1   yard/1 meter cotton twill tape, 1"/2.5 cm wide

Gauge:
20 stitches and 24 rows = 4"/10 cm in stockinette stitch

PANEL A:

Cast on 50 stitches with yarn A. Work in stockinette stitch (knit all right-side rows and purl all wrong-side rows) for 6 rows. Work an eyelet row: knit all stitches until the last 4 stitches, yarn over, knit 2 together, knit remaining 2 stitches. Work even for another 5 rows.

Begin four-row Fair Isle checkerboard pattern:

Row 1: Join yarn B and knit 2 stitches while carrying yarn A along the back of the piece; change back to yarn A and knit 2 stitches while carrying yarn B in the back. Repeat this 4-stitch pattern until 2 stitches remain, knit 2 stitches with yarn B.

Row 2: Purl 2 stitches with yarn B, purl 2 stitches with yarn A, and repeat until 2 stitches remain, purl 2 stitches with yarn B.

Row 3: Knit 2 stitches with yarn A, knit 2 stitches with yarn B, and repeat until 2 stitches remain, knit 2 stitches with yarn A.

Row 4: Purl 2 stitches with yarn A, purl 2 stitches with yarn B, and repeat until 2 stitches remain, purl 2 stitches with yarn A. Cut yarn B.

Continue with yarn A for 4 rows.

To shape the opening for the photo square, work for 19 stitches, bind off 12 stitches. Join a second ball of yarn A and work the remaining group of 19 stitches.

Work these two sections in stockinette stitch for 16 rows.

Next row: Work 19 stitches, cast on 12 stitches using the single cast-on method: make a loop with the working yarn and slip it over your left thumb with the end attached to the right needle closest to your fingers.

Hold the two ends of yarn in the palm of your left hand with your finger. Insert the needle under the end attached to the ball of yarn (which should be the one closest to your wrist) and pull upwards forming a small loop on the right needle. Pull this loop tight. Repeat until you have added 12 stitches. Work the stitches on the stitch holder to the end of the row.

Work for 3 rows. Repeat four Fair Isle rows. Work with yarn A only for another 4 rows. Work an eyelet row as before.

Work even for another 5 rows. Bind off.

PANEL B:
Cast on 50 stitches with yarn A. Work in stockinette stitch for 6 rows. Work an eyelet row as for Panel A. Knit all stitches until the last 4 stitches, yarn over, knit 2 together, knit remaining 2 stitches.

Work even for another 5 rows.

Work four-row Fair Isle checkerboard pattern.

Continue with yarn A only for 24 rows.

Repeat four-row Fair Isle checkerboard pattern.

Work with yarn A only for another 4 rows. Work an eyelet row as for Panel A.

Work even for another 5 rows. Bind off.

PANEL C:
Work as for Panel B, *except* for the two eyelet rows. Work Panel C eyelet rows as follows: knit 2 stitches, knit 2 together, yarn over, knit all remaining stitches.

Make two.

FINISHING:
Weave in all loose ends with the tapestry needle.

Disassemble the photo album by untying the ribbon and removing the front and back covers.

With the crochet hook and yarn B, work a single crochet around the edges of the photo square opening in Panel A.

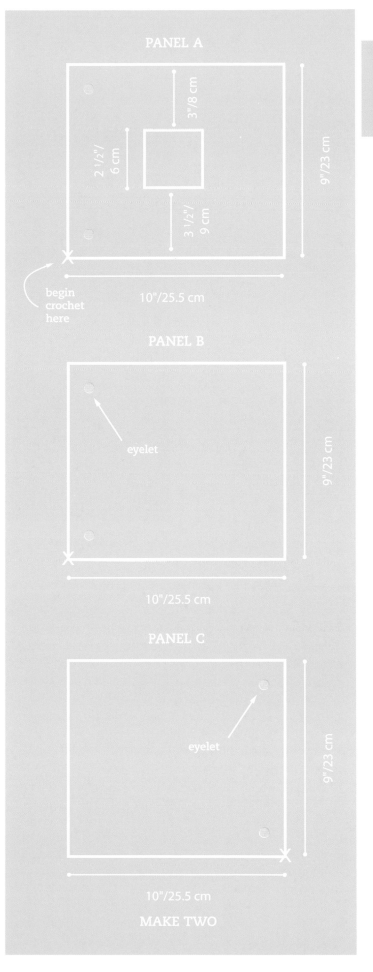

PANEL A

3"/8 cm

2 1/2"/6 cm

3 1/2"/9 cm

9"/23 cm

begin crochet here

10"/25.5 cm

PANEL B

eyelet

9"/23 cm

10"/25.5 cm

PANEL C

eyelet

9"/23 cm

10"/25.5 cm

MAKE TWO

Place Panel A on top of one Panel C with the wrong sides facing. With the crochet hook and yarn B, join three sides of the pieces together using single crochet. Start at one of the left-hand corners (see diagram) and work along the long (10"/25 cm) edge first, then the narrow (9"/23 cm) edge, and then the other long edge. Leave the other narrow edge open. Make sure that you work three single crochets on each corner so the cover will fit properly. *Do not bind off.*

Place a romantic photo or drawing in the photo holder on the inside of the front cover. Insert the front cover in between the two knitted panels. Stretch the two panels to fit the front cover and line up the eyelet holes with the holes in the front cover as your guides. Join the remaining edge with single crochet.

Place Panel B on top of the other Panel C with the wrong sides facing. With the crochet hook and yarn B, join

them with a single crochet stitch, working 3 crochet stitches in each corner and leaving one of the narrow edges unclosed. *Do not bind off.* Insert the back cover between the two panels with the outside of the photo album back cover facing the wrong side of Panel C. Line up the eyelet holes with the holes in the back cover, stretching the two panels to fit as you did with the front cover. Join the remaining edge with single crochet.

Cut a piece of cotton twill tape approximately 1 yard/1 meter long. Thread the cotton twill through the tapestry needle. Thread the tapestry needle through one of the eyelet holes in the front cover, the photo sheets, and the back cover. Insert it into the other eyelet hole on the back cover and up again through the photo sheets and the front cover. Tie the cotton twill tape into a bow on the top side of the album. Tie small knots at the end of the cotton twill tape and cut the tape very close to these knots.

Thank you
Marve ♥
Rebecca

7. charmed bracelet

Although this bracelet is knit in a very simple seed stitch, its silvery sparkle makes it dressy. The combination of a laced ribbon closure, a charm in a modern shape, and the old-fashioned knit creates a distinctive look. You can monogram the silver charm with each of your bridesmaids' initials for a wonderful gift. Or you could knit each bracelet in a different color yarn to match the bridesmaids' dresses. You could vary the charm—maybe you prefer a heart shape.

charmed bracelet

Experience Level:
Beginner

Size:
One size fits all

Finished Measurements:
2¼" × 5½"/6 cm × 14 cm

Yarns:
A: 1 ball Suss Perle Cotton (100% cotton; 2 ounces/57 grams; 256 yards/236 meters), color Silver Birch
B: 1 ball Suss Lurex (65% nylon/35% metallic; 1 ounce/29 grams; 225 yards/208 meters), color Silver

Notions:
1   pair size 3 (3.25 mm) needles
    tapestry needle
    40"/102 cm gray satin ribbon, ¼"/.5 cm wide
1   round silver charm, 1"/ 2.5 cm in diameter

Gauge:
24 stitches and 36 rows = 4"/10 cm in seed stitch

Since you will be working with two strands of yarn B, begin by dividing the yarn into two balls of equal size.

Cast on 13 stitches with one strand of yarn A and two strands of yarn B.

Work in seed stitch (see below) until piece measures 5½"/14 cm, or approximately 50 rows.

To work seed stitch with an odd number of stitches:

Row 1: Knit 1 stitch, purl 1 stitch, repeat until the end of the row.

Row 2: Repeat Row 1.

Bind off in seed stitch pattern.

FINISHING:
Weave in all loose ends with the tapestry needle.

Thread one end of the tapestry needle with the satin ribbon. Insert the needle into one of the corners of the knitted piece approximately 3 rows from the top and 3 stitches from the narrow (2¼"/6 cm) side edge. Pull the needle and ribbon through and insert, fold the knitted piece into a circular bracelet shape, and insert the needle into the corresponding corner of the opposite edge, 3 rows and 3 stitches from the edges. Lace the ribbon along the edge of the bracelet in a criss-cross shoelace pattern four times. The laces should be placed approximately ½"/1 cm apart (see photograph).

With one strand of yarn A and two strands of yarn B attach the silver charm to the bracelet at one of the corners.

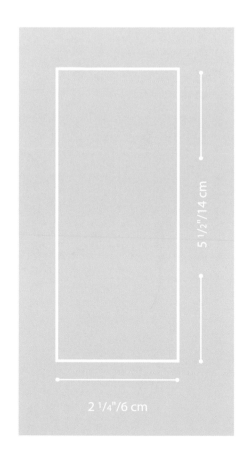

5 ½"/14 cm

2 ¼"/6 cm

8. maid-of-honor shrug

When you only need the slightest amount of coverage, shrugs are perfect. If you're having a spring or summer wedding and your maid of honor is wearing a barely-there dress, this shrug will come in handy should the day turn chilly—a shrug just covers your arms, so it's like wearing only sleeves and doesn't spoil the overall effect of a special dress. You knit it in one piece, so it could not be simpler. The pale mauve fuzzy alpaca gives it a very romantic look. Not only for maids of honor!

maid-of-honor shrug

Experience Level:
Intermediate

Size:
Medium/Large (up to chest 38"/96.5 cm)

Finished Measurements:
Approximately 7" × 64"/18 cm × 162.5 cm (see diagram)

Yarn:
4 skeins Suss Melange (50% polyamid/30% acrylic/20% alpaca; 1.5 ounces/43 grams; 153 yards/141 meters), color Sweet Rose

Notions:
1   pair size 8 (5 mm) needles
4   stitch markers
    large tapestry needle
    straight pins (optional)

Gauge:
22 stitches and 20 rows = 4"/10 cm in stockinette stitch

Cast on 38 stitches. Work in stockinette stitch (knit all right-side rows and purl all wrong-side rows), increasing 1 stitch at the beginning and end of every 20 rows 4 times—46 stitches, 80 rows total.

Continue in stockinette and increase 1 stitch at the beginning and end of every 4 rows 3 times—52 stitches, 92 rows total. Increase 1 stitch at the beginning and end of every 2 rows 11 times—74 stitches, 114 rows total. Place a stitch marker at the beginning and end of the row 21"/53.5 cm from the cast-on edge.

Work even for 18"/45.5 cm, or approximately 90 rows, ending with a wrong-side row.

Decrease 1 stitch at the beginning and end of every 2 rows 11 times—52 stitches total. *At the same time,* place stitch markers at the beginning and end of the row 2"/5 cm from the beginning of this decrease section. Decrease 1 stitch at the beginning and end of every 4 rows 3 times—46 stitches total.

Decrease 1 stitch at the beginning and end of the next row—44 stitches total. Decrease 1 stitch at the beginning and end of every 20 rows 3 times—38 stitches total. Work even for 19 rows.

Bind off loosely.

FINISHING:
Weave in all loose ends with the tapestry needle.

Thread the tapestry needle with two strands of yarn. Fold the shrug lengthwise with the right sides facing each other and, beginning at the cast-on edge, seam the sleeve together using backstitch. Stop seaming when you reach the stitch markers. You may find it helpful to pin the sleeve together first before seaming. To ensure that the seam stays secure, add a few reinforcing stitches at the end of the seam near the armhole.

Repeat the process for the other sleeve.

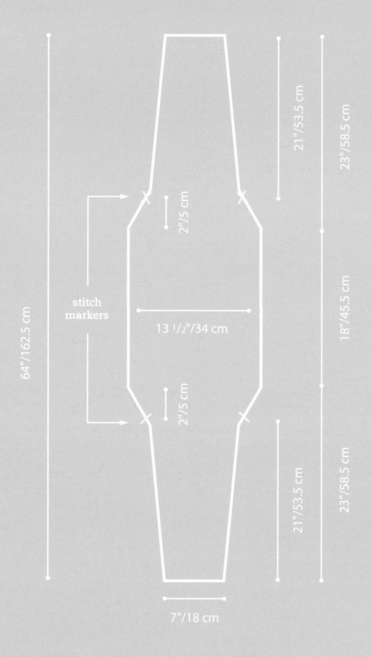

64"/162.5 cm

stitch
markers

2"/5 cm

13 1/2"/34 cm

2"/5 cm

7"/18 cm

21"/53.5 cm

23"/58.5 cm

18"/45.5 cm

23"/58.5 cm

21"/53.5 cm

9. bridesmaid wrap

When you're thinking about gifts for your bridesmaids, consider this wrap. It doesn't take much yarn, so it's economical enough to make for several girlfriends, yet it looks expensive and chic. It's such a practical present because your friends can wear it for the wedding and long afterwards as well. You can tie the wrap five different ways, making it one of the most versatile items you could ever knit. The sleeves are stockinette and the body is one-by-one rib, all in soft baby alpaca. Make one for each bridesmaid in a different color—and you might even want one for yourself!

bridesmaid wrap

Experience Level:
Intermediate

Size:
One size fits most

Finished Measurements:
Body: 21" wide × 80" long/53 cm × 203 cm
Sleeves: 25" long/63.5 cm (see diagram)

Yarn:
4 skeins Suss Fishnet (53% acrylic /30% nylon /17% alpaca; 1.5 ounces/43 grams;
285 yards/263 meters), color Mint

Notions:
1   pair size 11 circular knitting needles, 24"/61 cm long
1   pair size 9 knitting needles
    large tapestry needle
    straight pins (recommended)

Gauge:
16 stitches and 16 rows = 4"/10 cm in one-by-one rib stitch with size 11 needles
18 stitches and 20 rows = 4"/10 cm in stockinette stitch with size 9 needles
A note about gauge: Since Fishnet is such a thin yarn knitted on large needles, the
gauge for the rib stitch is a little difficult to pinpoint precisely. However, it is important
that the shoulder, armhole and sleeve measurements are consistent.

BODY:
Loosely cast on 84 stitches with the size 11 needles.
Work piece in a one-by-one rib (knit 1 stitch, purl
1 stitch, repeat until the end of the row) for 34"/85.5 cm.

Armhole Row 1: Work in rib for 26 stitches. Bind off the
next 32 stitches. Work the remaining 26 stitches.

Armhole Row 2: Work in rib for 26 stitches. Cast on
32 stitches as follows: Insert the right needle into the
space between the first two stitches on the left-hand
needle. Pull the yarn through, making a loop, and place
that loop back on the left needle. Work the remaining
26 stitches.

Continue in one-by-one rib for another 12"/30.5 cm.

Repeat the two Armhole Rows.

Work even for another 34"/85.5 cm, until piece measures
80"/203 cm from cast-on edge. Bind off loosely in rib
pattern.

SLEEVES:
Loosely cast on 36 stitches with the size 9 needles.
Work Sleeve in stockinette stitch (knit all right-side
rows and purl all wrong-side rows). Increase 1 stitch
at the beginning and end of every 8 rows 8 times—52
stitches total. Increase 1 stitch at the beginning and
end of every 6 rows 10 times—72 stitches total.

Bind off loosely. Make two Sleeves.

FINISHING:
Weave in any loose ends with the tapestry needle.

Sew up the Sleeve seams leaving a very small seam
allowance to maintain the light effect of the yarn. Pin
the Sleeves into the armholes. You may find it helpful
to turn the piece inside out to do this. Make sure you
pin the Sleeves evenly so there is no bunching or
stretching. Sew the Sleeves into the armholes.

Put your arms through the armholes and fold over the top edge of the body piece to make a collar. Let the bottom edge hang loosely, tie it around your waist, or throw one side over your shoulder. You could also accent it with a vintage shawl pin or brooch.

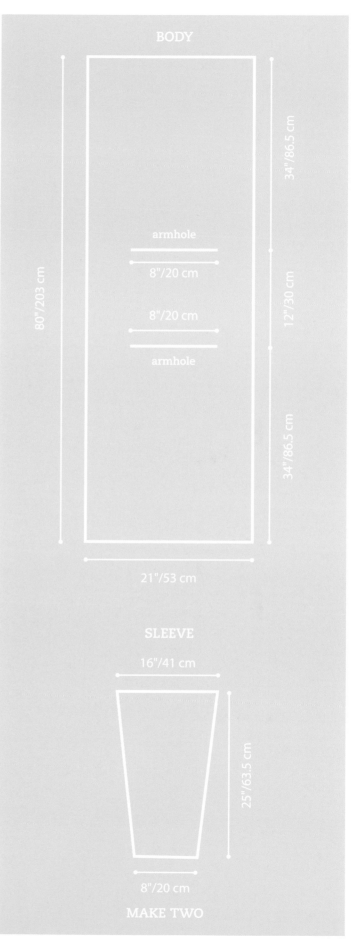

BODY

80"/203 cm

34"/86.5 cm

armhole

8"/20 cm

8"/20 cm

armhole

12"/30 cm

34"/86.5 cm

21"/53 cm

SLEEVE

16"/41 cm

25"/63.5 cm

8"/20 cm

MAKE TWO

10. ring cushion

Using a small pillow to carry precious jewels dates back to the Romans and Egyptians, who believed the wedding ring symbolized love with no beginning or end. Today, not everybody has a formal wedding complete with a ring bearer to carry the rings up the aisle. But even if you choose a simpler ceremony, you can still honor your rings by displaying them on the cushion at the altar or on a small table.

ring cushion

Experience Level:
Beginner

Finished Measurements:
8" × 8"/20.5 cm × 20.5 cm

Yarns:
2 skeins Suss Crystal (60% cotton/40% viscose; 1.5 ounces/43 grams; 90 yards/83 meters), color Ice Rose

Notions:
- 1 pair size 3 (3.25 mm) needles
  large tapestry needle
- 1 size B (2.25 mm) crochet hook
- 1 20-ounce bag polyester fiberfill
- 1 mother of pearl button, ½"/1 cm in diameter
- 1 pink pearl button, ½"/1 cm in diameter
- 1 yard/1 meter 100% white chiffon ribbon, 2"/5 cm wide

Gauge:
24 stitches and 30 rows = 4"/10 cm

CUSHION:

Cast on 48 stitches. Work in stockinette stitch (knit all right-side rows and purl all wrong-side rows) until piece measures 8"/20.5 cm, approximately 60 rows.

Bind off.

Make two.

FINISHING:

Weave in all loose ends with the tapestry needle.

Hold the two panels with wrong sides together. With the crochet hook, join the two cover panels with a single crochet stitch, leaving a 5"/13 cm opening on one side. Stuff the pillow with the polyester fiberfill until the pillow is plump and firm. The knitted stitches should stretch a little to accommodate the stuffing.

Close the opening using single crochet.

Crochet a shell-stitch border around all four edges of the pillow as follows:

Work 3 double crochet stitches into the same stitch, skip 3 stitches, work a slip stitch; repeat until you've worked around all four edges. Work an extra shell stitch at the corners of the pillow so the edging doesn't pull too tightly at the corners.

Thread the tapestry needle with the yarn and tie a knot at one end. Insert the needle and yarn into the center of the cushion (bottom side) and pull it through to the other side (top). Fold the chiffon ribbon in half and insert the needle into the center of the ribbon, through the shank of the pink pearl button, back again through the center of the ribbon, and through the center of the cushion. Thread the needle through the mother-of-pearl button to attach it to the bottom of the cushion, and pull the needle through to the top side again. Thread the yarn through the ribbon and the pink pearl button one more time and through the mother-of-pearl button on the bottom side. Pull the yarn taut to create an indentation. Repeat the process once more to anchor the buttons and tie off the yarn.

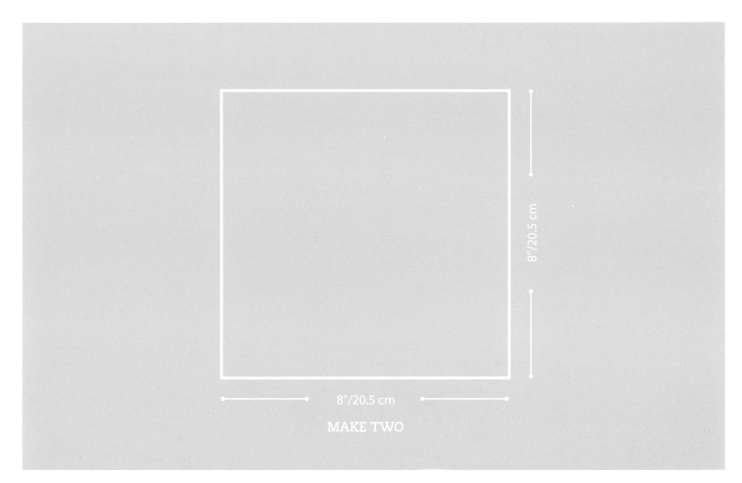

8"/20.5 cm

8"/20.5 cm

MAKE TWO

11. mother-of-the-bride handkerchief

A dainty handkerchief is the traditional gift for the mother of the bride. She will no doubt be dabbing away a tear or two during the wedding, after all. Traditional Swedish cross-stitch embroidery was my inspiration for this design. In Sweden my grandmother embroidered on top of everything she knit! The pearl-white cotton is quick to knit in stockinette and the wide crocheted lace trim is a sweet contrast. Consider knitting an extra for the mother of the groom for a good start to in-law relations.

mother-of-the-bride handkerchief

Experience Level:
Beginner

Finished Measurements:
11" × 11"/28 cm × 28 cm

Yarns:
A: 1 ball Suss Perle Cotton (100% cotton; 2 ounces/57 grams; 256 yards/236 meters), color Pure White
B: 1 skein Suss Silk (100% silk; 1.5 ounces/43 grams; 163 yards/150 meters), color Something Borrowed

Notions:
1   pair size 3 (3.25 mm) needles
large tapestry needle
1   size C (2.75 mm) crochet hook
sewing pins

Gauge:
32 stitches and 36 rows = 4"/10 cm in stockinette stitch with size 3 needles

Cast on 88 stitches with yarn A. Work in stockinette stitch (knit all right-side rows and purl all wrong-side rows) until handkerchief measures 11"/28 cm, or approximately 100 rows. Since you are working small stitches in cotton, pay careful attention to your tension and try to keep it nice and even as you work.

Bind off.

FINISHING:
Weave in any loose ends with the tapestry needle.

With the crochet hook and yarn B, work a single crochet around all four edges starting at one corner of the handkerchief. When you've worked all the way around the edges of the handkerchief, switch to yarn A, chain 3 stitches, and begin working fantail edging pattern in the hole of the second single crochet stitch from the corner.

Fantail edging: *work a triple crochet (yarn over 2 times, insert hook, yarn over, pull through stitch and then pull through 2 loops 3 times) twice, chain 3, insert hook in the first of the 3 chain stitches and pull yarn through this hole and loop on hook, chain 1, work 2 triple crochets in same hole as first 2. Chain 2, skip 2 single crochet edging stitches, triple crochet, chain 2, skip 2 single crochet edging stitches* and repeat from * to * until you have worked around entire edge of the handkerchief. Work an extra fantail at the corners of the handkerchief.

With the tapestry needle and yarn B, embroider the mother of the bride's initials in one of the corners of the handkerchief using chain stitch. You can draw your own alphabet or find an alphabet from a book. Copy the letters onto a piece of tracing paper, pin the paper to the corner of the handkerchief, and stitch over the outlines of the letters. When you are done embroidering, simply tear away the tracing paper. Any leftover scraps can be removed with tweezers.

With the tapestry needle and yarn B, use straight stitches and lazy daisy stitches to embroider four small star flowers (approximately ½"/1 cm each) at random in the same corner of the handkerchief as the initial (see photograph for placement suggestions). If you wish, you can photocopy the example model provided or copy it onto tracing paper to use the same technique you used for the initials.

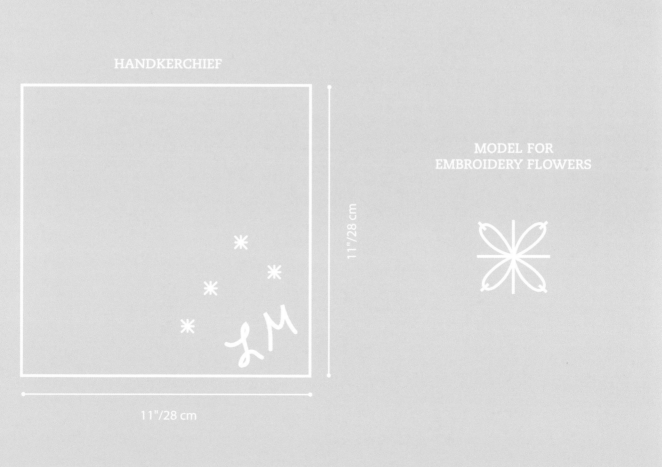

HANDKERCHIEF

𝓛 M

11"/28 cm

11"/28 cm

MODEL FOR
EMBROIDERY FLOWERS

2

for the
bride

Just as the bride has been waiting her whole life for her wedding day, I know this is the part you couldn't wait to get to! Every pattern is for the bride and her big day, from the Ultimate Wedding Dress, the most challenging, to a simple but extraordinary Classic Long Veil. The bridal gown is very slinky and form fitting, with lots of ruffles, and uses different yarns for different parts of the dress for even more interest. ✳ You have a choice of two pretty little handbags to knit for the wedding. A Tasseled Silk Bridal Purse is made in hand-dyed silk yarn and an open knit, then lined in a luxurious silk dupioni. I designed the Pouf Bridal Purse with a white iridescent nylon yarn that makes it look to me like a perfect tiny snowball. ✳ I know a bride whose best friend made her wedding dress in lieu of a regular wedding present. These larger projects would also make wonderful bridal shower gifts if you know someone getting married. But you probably shouldn't try to surprise the bride! Make it a special time for the two of you to share, and your friendship will stay and grow stronger than ever even after her wedding.

12. ultimate wedding dress

This one-of-a-kind bridal gown fits like a glove. The knit fabric clings smoothly to the body, while the silk top has graceful wide sleeves that end with a ruffle. Austrian crystal trim sparkles as brightly as any bride. It's sophisticated yet a bit bohemian. When I was designing it, I pictured it on a barefoot bride standing on fresh green grass in a beautiful garden setting. The dress definitely requires an investment of time to make, but isn't your wedding day worth it? I also suggest you try it in other colors for important social events. With its beautiful neckline, it makes an incredible party dress.

ultimate wedding dress

Experience Level:
Advanced

Sizes:
Small (medium, large)

Finished Measurements:
Chest: 31" (33", 35")/79 (84, 89) cm
Length (hanging): 57" (58", 60")/145 (147, 152.5) cm

Yarns:
A: 12 skeins Suss Star (90% viscose/10% nylon; 1.5 ounces/43 grams; 126 yards/ 116 meters), color White
B: 11 skeins Suss Crisp (60% viscose/25% acrylic/10% nylon/5% alpaca; 1.5 ounces/ 43 grams; 137 yards/126 meters), color Pearl
C: 3 skeins Suss Silk (100% silk; 1.5 ounces/43 grams; 163 yards/150 meters), color Mother of Pearl

Notions:
1   pair size 5 (3.75 mm) circular needles, 32"/81 long
1   pair size 10½ (6.5 mm) circular needles, 40"/100 cm long
1   pair size 7 (4.5 mm) needles
1   knitting row counter (highly recommended)
1   stitch holder
    large tapestry needle
    sewing pins
    80"/203 cm white satin ribbon, 2½"/6.5 cm wide
    sewing needle and ivory sewing thread
48 4 mm clear Austrian crystal beads
10 6 mm clear Austrian crystal beads
8   round pearl buttons with shanks, ⅝"/1.5 cm in diameter
    7"/18 cm invisible zipper (optional)

Gauge:
24 stitches and 30 rows = 4"/10cm in stockinette stitch with size 5 needles and yarn A
14 stitches and 18 rows = 4"/10 cm in stockinette stitch with size 10½ needles and yarn B
24 stitches and 28 rows = 4"/10 cm in stockinette stitch with size 7 needles and yarn C

SKIRT BACK:
Cast on 112 (118, 124) stitches with yarn A and size 5 needles. Add 4 stitches at the beginning of every row for 14 rows—168 (174, 180) stitches total.

Decrease 1 stitch at the beginning and end of every 5 rows 45 times—78 (84, 90) stitches total.

Bind off.

SKIRT FRONT:
Work as for Skirt Back until bind-off row, but do not bind off.

Bind off 3 stitches at the beginning of every row 10 (12, 14) times—48 (48, 48) stitches total. Decrease 1 stitch at the beginning and end of every row 22 (22, 22) times— 4 (4, 4) stitches.

Bind off.

SLEEVES:
Cast on 84 (84, 90) stitches with yarn A and the size 5 needles. Work in stockinette stitch (knit all right-side rows and purl all wrong-side rows). Decrease 1 stitch at the beginning and end of every 11 (12, 12) rows 9 (9, 9) times—66 (66, 72) stitches total. Work even until sleeve

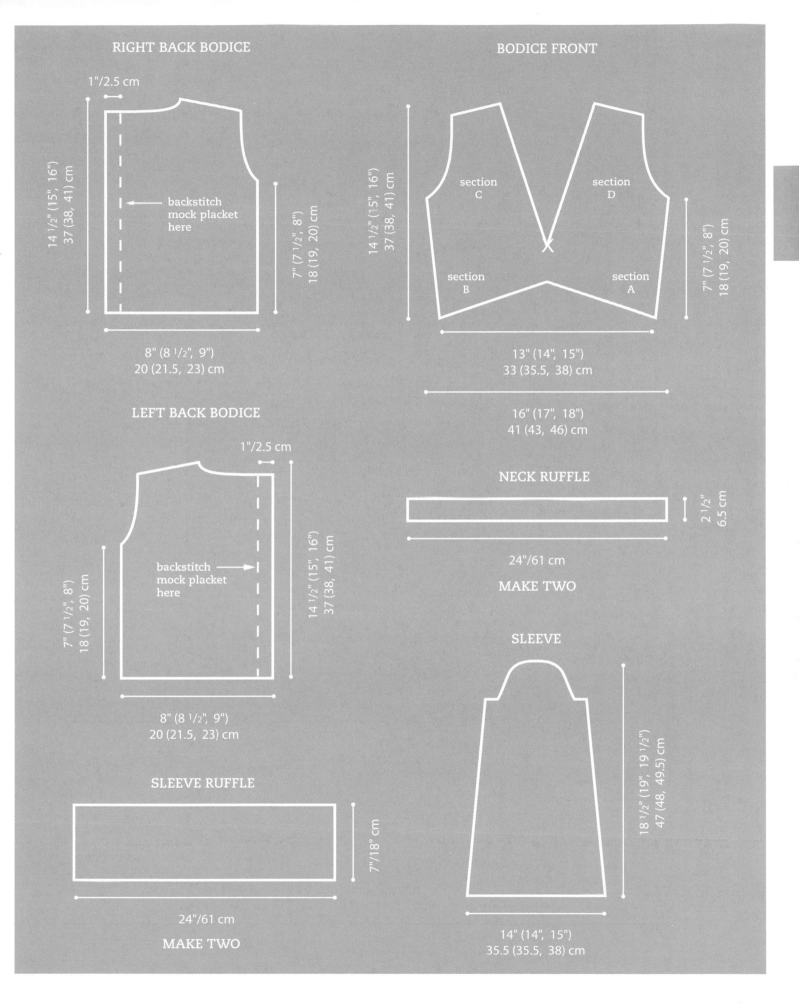

RIGHT BACK BODICE

1"/2.5 cm

14 1/2" (15", 16")
37 (38, 41) cm

backstitch mock placket here

7" (7 1/2", 8")
18 (19, 20) cm

8" (8 1/2", 9")
20 (21.5, 23) cm

LEFT BACK BODICE

1"/2.5 cm

backstitch mock placket here

7" (7 1/2", 8")
18 (19, 20) cm

14 1/2" (15", 16")
37 (38, 41) cm

8" (8 1/2", 9")
20 (21.5, 23) cm

SLEEVE RUFFLE

7"/18" cm

24"/61 cm

MAKE TWO

BODICE FRONT

section C

section D

section B

section A

14 1/2" (15", 16")
37 (38, 41) cm

7" (7 1/2", 8")
18 (19, 20) cm

13" (14", 15")
33 (35.5, 38) cm

16" (17", 18")
41 (43, 46) cm

NECK RUFFLE

2 1/2"
6.5 cm

24"/61 cm

MAKE TWO

SLEEVE

18 1/2" (19", 19 1/2") cm
47 (48, 49.5) cm

14" (14", 15")
35.5 (35.5, 38) cm

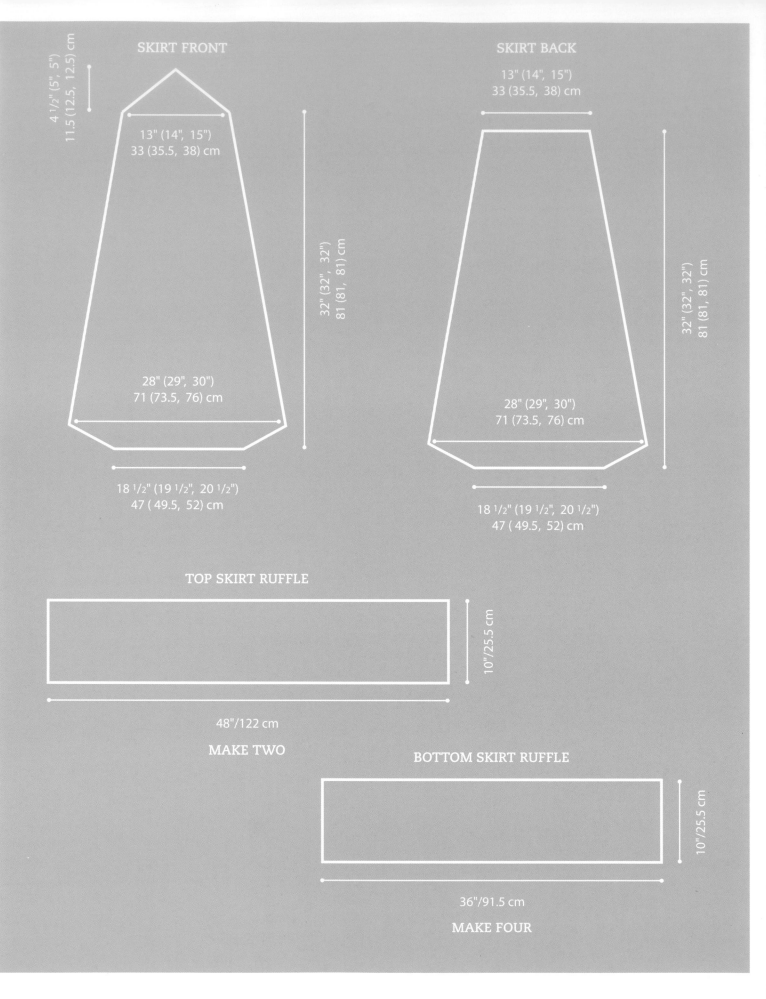

SKIRT FRONT

4 1/2" (5", 5")
11.5 (12.5, 12.5) cm

13" (14", 15")
33 (35.5, 38) cm

32" (32", 32")
81 (81, 81) cm

28" (29", 30")
71 (73.5, 76) cm

18 1/2" (19 1/2", 20 1/2")
47 (49.5, 52) cm

SKIRT BACK

13" (14", 15")
33 (35.5, 38) cm

32" (32", 32")
81 (81, 81) cm

28" (29", 30")
71 (73.5, 76) cm

18 1/2" (19 1/2", 20 1/2")
47 (49.5, 52) cm

TOP SKIRT RUFFLE

10"/25.5 cm

48"/122 cm

MAKE TWO

BOTTOM SKIRT RUFFLE

10"/25.5 cm

36"/91.5 cm

MAKE FOUR

measures 14½" (15", 15½")/37 (38, 39) cm from cast-on edge.

To shape armholes, bind off 5 stitches at the beginning of the next 2 rows—56 (56, 62) stitches total. Decrease 1 stitch at the beginning and end of every other row 12 times—32 (32, 38) stitches. Decrease 1 stitch at the beginning and end of every row 5 times—22 (22, 28) stitches.

Bind off. Make two.

NECK RUFFLE:
Cast on 84 stitches loosely with yarn B and size 10½ needles. Work in stockinette until piece measures 2½"/6.5 cm, or 12 rows.

Bind off loosely. Make two.

SLEEVE RUFFLE:
Cast on 84 stitches loosely with yarn B and size 10½ needles. Work in stockinette until piece measures 7"/18 cm, or 32 rows.

Bind off loosely. Make two.

TOP SKIRT RUFFLE:
Cast on 168 stitches loosely with yarn B and size 10½ needles. Work in stockinette until piece measures 10"/25 cm, or 45 rows.

Bind off loosely. Make two.

BOTTOM SKIRT RUFFLE:
Cast on 126 stitches with yarn B and size 10½ needles. Work in stockinette until piece measures 10"/25.5 cm, or 45 rows.

Bind off loosely. Make four.

BODICE FRONT:
Section A:
Cast on 3 (5, 5) stitches with yarn C and size 7 needles. Work in stockinette stitch. Increases will be done at different rates on the bottom edge and side-seam edge. For section A, the side-seam edge will be the right edge when the right side of the piece is facing you and the bottom edge will be the left edge when the right side of the piece is facing you.

Increase 1 stitch every row on the skirt edge 30 (30, 32)

times. *At the same time*, increase 1 stitch every 7 rows on the side-seam edge. Place these 37 (39, 41) stitches on a stitch holder.

Section B:
Cast on 3 (5, 5) stitches with yarn C and size 7 needles. Work in stockinette stitch. For section B, the side-seam edge will be the left edge when the right side of the piece is facing you and the bottom edge will be the right edge when the right side of the piece is facing you.

Increase 1 stitch every row on the skirt edge 30 (30, 32) times. *At the same time*, increase 1 stitch every 7 rows on the side-seam edge—37 (39, 41) stitches total.

When you have worked all 30 (30, 32) rows, work another row and join stitches from stitch holder—74 (78, 82) stitches total. Work for 7 rows, continuing the pattern of side seam increases (1 stitch every 7 rows) on both edges—76 (80, 84) stitches.

Purl 38 (40, 42) stitches and place remaining 38 (40, 42) stitches on stitch holder.

Section C:
For section C, the neckline edge will be the right edge when the right side of the piece is facing you and the armhole edge will be the left edge when the right side of the piece is facing you.

Continue the pattern of side seam increases on the left edge until armhole shaping. Decrease 1 stitch every 4 rows on the right edge (neckline) until bind off. Work until piece measures 7" (7½", 8")/18 (19, 20) cm from cast-on edge.

To shape armhole, bind off 4 stitches at the beginning of the next wrong-side row. Decrease 1 stitch at the beginning of every wrong-side row 3 times. Work until piece measures 13¾" (14¼", 15¼")/35 (36, 39) cm.

Bind off 5 (6, 6) stitches at the beginning of the next 3 wrong-side rows. Work one row. Bind off remaining stitches.

Section D:
For section D, the neckline edge will be the left edge when the right side of the piece is facing you and the armhole edge will be the right edge when the right side of the piece is facing you.

Work from the stitches on the stitch holder and continue the pattern of side seam increases on the right edge until armhole shaping. Decrease 1 stitch every 4 rows on the left edge (neckline) until bind off. Work until piece measures 7" (7½", 8")/18 (19, 20) cm from cast on edge.

To shape armhole, bind off 4 stitches at the beginning of the next right-side row. Decrease 1 stitch at the beginning of every right-side row 3 times. Work until piece measures 13¾" (14¼", 15¼")/35 (36, 39) cm.

Bind off 5 (6, 6) stitches at the beginning of the next 3 right-side rows. Work one row. Bind off remaining stitches.

RIGHT BACK BODICE:

Cast on 48 (52, 54) stitches with yarn C and size 7 needles. Work in stockinette stitch until piece measures 7" (8", 8½")/18 (19, 20) cm.

Bind off 4 stitches at the beginning of the next right-side row—44 (48, 50) stitches. Decrease 1 stitch at the beginning of every right-side row 3 times—41 (45, 47) stitches. Work even until the piece measures 13¾" (14¼", 15 ¼")/35 (36, 39) cm.

Bind off 17 stitches at the beginning of the next wrong-side row—24 (28, 30) stitches. Bind off 5 (6, 6) stitches at the beginning of the next 3 right-side rows. *At the same time,* bind off 2 (2, 3) stitches at the beginning of the next 2 wrong-side rows.

Bind off remaining 5 (6, 6) stitches.

LEFT BACK BODICE:

Cast on 48 (52, 54) stitches with yarn C and size 7 needles. Work in stockinette stitch until piece measures 7" (8", 8½")/18 (19, 20) cm.

Bind off 4 stitches at the beginning of the next wrong-side row—44 (48, 50) stitches. Decrease 1 stitch at the beginning of every wrong-side row 3 times 41 (45, 47) stitches. Work even until the piece measures 13¾" (14¼", 15¼")/35 (36, 39) cm.

Bind off 17 stitches at the beginning of the next right-side row—24 (28, 30) stitches. Bind off 5 (6, 6) stitches at the beginning of the next 3 wrong-side rows. *At the same time,* bind off 2 (2, 3) stitches at the beginning of the next 2 right-side rows.

Bind off remaining 5 (6, 6) stitches.

FINISHING:

Weave in all loose ends with the tapestry needle.

note The following instructions are for hand-sewing the Ultimate Wedding Dress. If you have access to a sewing machine, you can easily do all the seams on the machine instead.

BODICE ASSEMBLY:

To form the mock placket for the buttons, place the Left Back Bodice and the Right Back Bodice together with the right sides facing up and the left edge of the Right Back Bodice overlapping the right edge of the Left Back Bodice by 1"/2.5 cm (see diagram). Pin the two pieces together and, with the tapestry needle and yarn C, use very small stitches to backstitch the two side edges to the corresponding bodice piece making one bodice back piece.

Cut the satin ribbon into two lengths of 40"/101.5 cm. With the sewing needle and thread, sew one length of ribbon one of the side seams of the back bodice piece at the cast-on edge, leaving a ¼"/1 cm seam allowance. Repeat for the other back bodice side seam and the other length of ribbon. Pin and, with the tapestry needle and yarn C, sew together the shoulder seams and side seams of the bodice using backstitch.

This dress should be very easy to slip into, but if you want more flexibility, you can add a 7"/18 cm invisible zipper to one of the side seams of the bodice.

With the sewing needle and thread, sew together the narrow ends of the two Neck Ruffles leaving a ¼"/1 cm seam allowance and anchor this seam to the center of the bottom of the neckline (see "X" on diagram of Bodice Front). With the sewing needle and thread, tack the other two ends of the Neck Ruffle to the back of the neck at the edges of the button placket. Work a very loose basting stitch along the edges of the ruffles nearest the neckline. Pin the Neck Ruffles to the neckline edge finessing the gathers by pulling the loose basting stitch as you go. You can cut the basting thread when you are done pinning. Sew the Neck Ruffle to the neckline using very small stitches.

Pin together the sleeve seams and, with the sewing needle and thread, sew together the sleeve seams using backstitch.

With the sewing needle and thread, sew together the two side seams of the Sleeve Ruffles to form a tube. With the tapestry needle and yarn B, work a loose running stitch along one of the edges of one tube and gather it until the circumference is 14" (14", 15")/35.5 (35.5, 38) cm. Pin this edge to the edge of the cuff of one of the sleeves. With the sewing needle and thread, sew the ruffle to the cuff. Repeat for the other ruffle and sleeve.

Pin the sleeves into the armholes and, with the sewing needle and thread, sew the sleeves into the armholes using backstitch.

SKIRT ASSEMBLY:

Place the Skirt Front and the Skirt Back together with the right sides facing each other and pin the side seams. With the sewing needle and thread, sew the two side seams together using backstitch.

Pin together the bodice and the skirt, making sure that you match up the side seams as well as the center of the bodice and Skirt Front. With the sewing needle and thread, sew the bodice and skirt together securely using backstitch.

With the same basting stitch and pinning method you used for the neckline ruffle, attach one of the Top Skirt Ruffle pieces to the front of the skirt approximately 6"/15 cm from the bottom edge. Repeat with the other Top Skirt Ruffle piece on the back of the skirt. With the sewing needle and thread, sew together the side seams of the two Top Skirt Ruffles.

With the sewing needle and thread, sew together the side edges of two of the Bottom Ruffle pieces. Using the same method as for the Top Skirt Ruffle, gather this Bottom Ruffle and sew it to the bottom edge of the front of the skirt. Repeat for the back of the skirt. Sew together the side seams of the Bottom Ruffles.

EMBELLISHMENTS:

Mark the placement of the 10 6-mm beads with sewing pins spaced evenly about 1¾"/4.5 cm apart along the front of the bodice on the border between the bodice and the skirt (see photograph for placement suggestions). When you are satisfied with their placement, use the sewing needle and thread to attach the beads.

After determining proper placement using sewing pins, attach 10 4-mm Austrian crystal beads evenly (about 1½"/4 cm apart) to the cuff of each sleeve. After determining proper placement using sewing pins, attach 28 4-mm Austrian crystals evenly (about 2½"/6.5 cm apart) to the skirt at the border between the top ruffle and the skirt.

After determining proper placement using sewing pins, attach the decorative pearl buttons to the placket on the back of the bodice. The first button should be centered about ½"/1 cm from the back neck edge and the rest of the buttons should be about 2"/5 cm apart.

Fold over the ends of the satin ribbon ¼"/1 cm twice. Pin and, with the sewing needle and thread, whipstitch this hem to the ribbon using very small stitches. Tie the ribbon together loosely in a bow.

13. classic long veil

If you want to look like a fairy-tale bride, this traditional-length veil would be a good choice. Randomly scattered iridescent sequins give a modern twist to an old-fashioned look. The knitted veil falls from a headband you make by braiding cotton yarn and then wrapping it with ribbon. Ivory ribbon roses are the finishing touch.

classic long veil

Experience Level:
Intermediate

Size:
One size fits all

Finished Measurements:
Veil: 36" wide × 56" long/91.5 × 142 cm
Headband: circumference 21"/53.5 cm

Yarns:
A: 4 skeins Suss Handpaint Mohair (70% kid mohair/30% silk; 0.9 ounces/26 grams;
230 yards/212 meters), color Ivory
B: 1 skein Suss Cotton (100% cotton; 2.5 ounces/71 grams; 118 yards/109 meters),
color Naturale

Notions:
- 1 pair size 11 (8 mm) circular needles, 32"/80 cm long
  large tapestry needle
  sewing pins
- 2 yards rayon ribbon, 1"/2.5 cm wide, color ivory
- 12 ribbon roses, color ivory
  sewing needle and ivory thread
- 40 white iridescent sequins

Gauge:
14 stitches and 16 rows = 4"/10 cm in stockinette stitch

Cast on 56 stitches loosely. Work in stockinette stitch (knit all right-side rows and purl all wrong-side rows), for 1 row even. Continue in stockinette, increasing 1 stitch at the beginning of every right-side row and the end of every wrong-side row for 20 rows—76 stitches total. Add 8 stitches at the beginning of every 6 right-side rows 6 times—124 stitches.

Work even until piece measures 42"/107 cm from cast-on edge.

Bind off 8 stitches at the beginning of every 6 rows 6 times—76 stitches. Decrease 1 stitch at the beginning of every right-side row and the end of every wrong-side row for 20 rows—56 stitches.

Bind off *loosely*.

FINISHING:
Weave in all loose ends with a tapestry needle.

To make the circlet headpiece, cut 30 lengths of yarn B approximately 40"/101.5 cm each and line up the ends evenly. Tie a knot at one end, trimming the ends to about ½"/1 cm from the knot. Divide these lengths into 3 groups of 10 each and braid them together until you have a braid 21"/53.5 cm long. Tie a knot at this end of the braid and trim the ends about ½"/1 cm from the knot.

Fold this braid in half loosely so the two ends overlap about 1"/2.5 cm and the braid forms a circle. Tie these two ends together by wrapping a piece of yarn B tightly around the two knotted ends and tying it off.

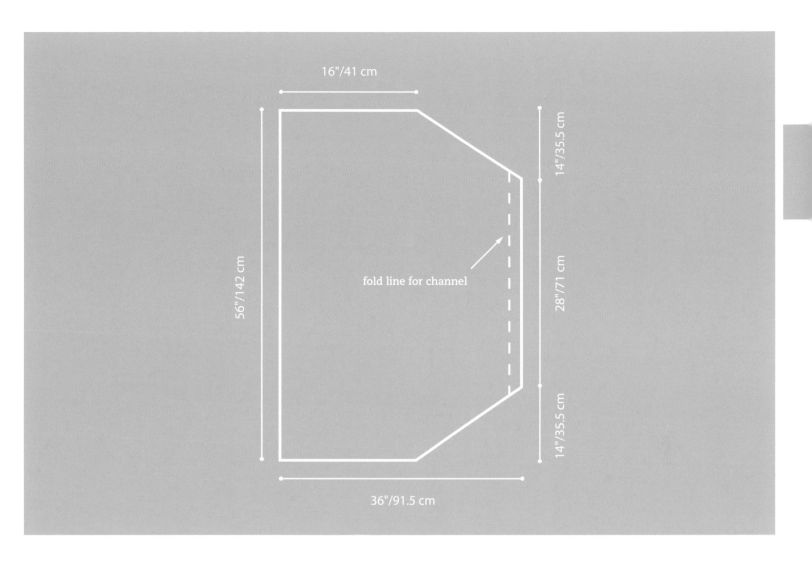

16"/41 cm

56"/142 cm

14"/35.5 cm

28"/71 cm

14"/35.5 cm

fold line for channel

36"/91.5 cm

Pin one end of the rayon ribbon to the inside of the braided circle at this knotted join. Wrap the ribbon over and over again around the entire circle of the braid (see photograph). Remove the pin, tie the two ends of ribbon together in a small knot, and trim the ribbon close to the two knot ends.

With the sewing needle and thread, attach the ribbon roses to the braided circle about 1"/2.5 cm apart. You may find it helpful to place sewing pins evenly around the braid to mark where you want to place the ribbon roses.

To make a channel to gather the veil, fold over the narrow (28"/71 cm) side edge of the veil (see diagram) approximately 1"/2.5 cm towards the wrong side of the veil. Pin this channel to the wrong side of the veil. With the tapestry needle and yarn A, start at the beginning of one end of the channel and whipstitch it to the wrong

side of the veil. *Do not tie off the yarn* when you reach the other end of the channel. With the yarn remaining on the tapestry needle, insert the needle into the end of the channel and gather until the channel is only 8"/20 cm long. Tie off the yarn at the "starting point" of the channel to hold the gather loosely in place.

Fold this gathered edge in half and place a pin at this center point. Line up this pin with the center back of the braided circlet headpiece (the point where the two knotted ends of the braid meet). Pin the gathered edge evenly to the inside of the braided circle with the gathered edge extending 4"/10 cm from the marker pin in both directions. With the tapestry needle and yarn A, whipstitch the gathered edge to the braided circle.

With the sewing needle and thread, attach the 40 white iridescent sequins to the outside (knit side) of the veil randomly, about 4-6"/10-15 cm apart from each other.

14. waterfall veil

The length and full shape of this veil make it perfect for a shorter wedding dress. When the tulle piece is in front of your face, it really does look like a waterfall. The back section is knit in a gorgeous pattern called cloverleaf lace, then trimmed in fantail crochet. A simple comb holds the whole thing in place but is not visible.

waterfall veil

Experience Level:
Intermediate

Size:
One size fits all

Finished Measurements:
35" wide × 23" long/89 cm × 58 cm (without crochet edging)

Yarns:
A: 2 skeins Suss Handpaint Mohair (70% kid mohair/30% silk; 0.9 ounces/26 grams; 230 yards/212 meters), color Rose
B: 1 skein Suss Web (53% acrylic/30% nylon/17% alpaca; 0.9 ounces/26 grams; 339 yards/313 meters), color Ivory

Notions:
1   pair size 11 (8 mm) circular needles, 32"/81 cm long
    large tapestry needle
1   size G (4 mm) crochet hook
    piece of tulle 40" wide × 80" long/101.5 × 203 cm
1   metal hair comb, 3½"/9 cm wide

Gauge:
14 stitches and 16 rows = 4"/10 cm in stockinette stitch

With one strand of yarn A and one strand of yarn B, cast on 124 stitches loosely. Work in stockinette stitch (knit all right-side rows and purl all wrong-side rows) for 6 rows.

Begin 16-row Cloverleaf Lace Pattern and work until piece measures 17"/43 cm from cast-on edge, or approximately 68 rows.

CLOVERLEAF LACE PATTERN:
Row 1: Knit 5 stitches, [yarn over, slip 1 stitch as if to knit, knit 2 together, pass slipped stitch over first (leftmost) stitch on right needle, yarn over, knit 5 stitches], repeat until last 7 stitches; yarn over, slip 1 stitch as if to knit, knit 2 together, pass slipped stitch over first stitch on right needle, knit remaining 4 stitches.

Row 2: Purl all stitches.

Row 3: Knit 6 stitches, [yarn over, slip 1 stitch as if to knit, knit 1, pass slipped stitch over first stitch on right needle, knit 6 stitches], repeat until last 6 stitches; yarn over, slip 1 stitch as if to knit, knit 1, pass slipped stitch over first stitch on right needle, knit remaining 4 stitches.

Rows 5 and 7: Purl all stitches.

Rows 4, 6, and 8: Knit all stitches.

Row 9: Knit 4 stitches, [knit 5 stitches, yarn over, slip 1 stitch as if to knit, knit 2 together, pass slipped stitch over first stitch on right needle, yarn over], repeat until last 8 stitches, knit 8 stitches.

Row 10: Purl all stitches.

Row 11: Knit 10 stitches, [yarn over, slip 1 stitch as if to knit, knit 1, pass slipped stitch over first stitch on right needle, knit 6 stitches], repeat until last 2 stitches, knit 2 stitches.

Rows 12, 14, and 16: Purl all stitches.

Rows 13 and 15: Knit all stitches.

When the piece is 17"/43 cm from cast-on edge, begin decreasing 1 stitch at the beginning and end of every row for 24 rows while maintaining Cloverleaf Lace Pattern—76 stitches total.

VEIL

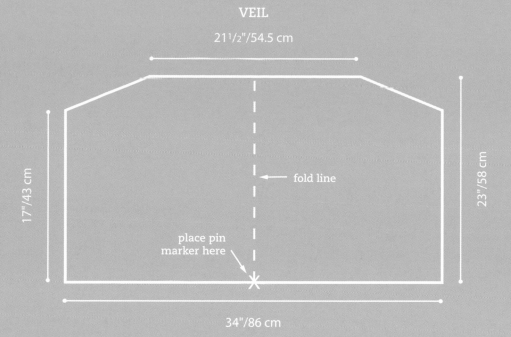

21¹/₂"/54.5 cm

17"/43 cm

23"/58 cm

← fold line

place pin
marker here

✕

34"/86 cm

Please note that these two diagrams are not
drawn to scale.

TULLE

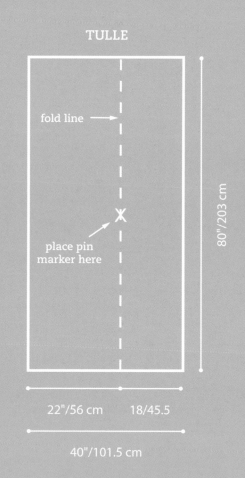

fold line →

✕

place pin
marker here

80"/203 cm

22"/56 cm

18/45.5

40"/101.5 cm

Bind off loosely.

Weave in all loose ends with the tapestry needle.

Fold the tulle lengthwise 22"/56 cm in from the edge. Fold it again widthwise to find the center point and mark that spot with a pin (see diagram). Thread the tapestry needle with one strand of yarn A and one strand of yarn B approximately 2 yards/2 meters long. Leaving a tail approximately 10"/25 cm long (do not pull the yarn all the way through), work a running stitch along the lengthwise fold starting at a point about 24"/61 cm from the pin and ending at another point about 24"/61 cm on the other side of the pin. Pull the yarn like a pair of drawstrings to gather the tulle until it is 3½"/9 cm long and secure it tightly at both ends. Do not remove the pin.

Fold the veil in half lengthwise (see diagram). To mark the place where the center of the hair comb will be attached, place a pin at the center of the cast-on edge. With the tapestry needle and one strand of yarn A and one strand of yarn B, work a running stitch along this edge, gather it until it is 3½"/9 cm long, and secure the ends tightly as you did with the tulle. Do not remove the pin.

Place the veil right-side up on top of the 22"/56 cm section of the tulle. Use the pin markers to line up the centers of the gathers. Pin the veil and the tulle together at their center points and pin the edges of the knitted veil to the tulle placing the pins about 6"/15 cm apart. Do not remove the pins.

With the tapestry needle and one strand of yarn A and one strand of yarn B, attach the center of the straight edge of the hair comb to the tulle and knitted veil at the center points marked by the pins. Work outward from the center and whipstitch the veil and tulle securely to the hair comb. Remove the center marker pins only.

Lay the veil down as flat as possible with the tulle side facing up. Trim all four corners of the tulle to match the rounded corners of the knitted piece.

With the crochet hook and one strand of yarn A and one strand of yarn B, work a single crochet around the entire edge of the veil, including the gathered edge attached to the hair comb. When you return to the starting point of your crochet, work in fantail pattern twice around the entire edge as well. At the hair comb, the crochet edging will stand up like a tiara.

Chain 3 stitches and, in the second single crochet edging stitch, *work a triple crochet (yarn over 2 times, insert hook, yarn over, pull through stitch and then pull through 2 loops 3 times) twice, chain 3, insert hook in the first of the 3 chain stitches and pull yarn through this hole and loop on hook, chain 1, work 2 triple crochets in same hole as first two. Chain 2, skip 2 single crochet edging stitches, triple crochet, chain 2, skip 2 single crochet edging stitches* and repeat from * to * until you have worked around entire edge of the knitted veil.

At the end of the first round of fantail edging, slip stitch to join the round, chain 4 stitches, and work the fantail edge pattern around the veil a second time.

15. rehearsal dinner bolero top

Knit in a 100% silk yarn, this top has raglan sleeves and a nice curve around the bodice. Beautiful French lace and freshwater pearls dress it up for your festive rehearsal dinner. Plus, you don't have to buy a whole new outfit: this lovely top added to a simple sleeveless linen or silk dress you already own will make you feel extra special the night before your wedding.

rehearsal dinner bolero top

Experience Level:
Advanced

Sizes:
Small (medium, large, extra large)
Chest: 34" (36", 38", 40")/86 (91, 96.5, 101.5) cm
Length: 15" (16", 17", 18")/38 (41, 43, 46) cm

Yarn:
4 skeins Suss Silk (100% silk; 1.5 ounces/43 grams; 163 yards/150 meters), color Rose Bouquet

Notions:
1   pair size 3 (3.25 mm) circular needles, 24"/61 cm long
     knitting row counter
4   stitch markers
     large tapestry needle
     sewing needle and ecru sewing thread
3½ yards/3.5 meters ecru French lace, 1"/2.5 cm wide
12 freshwater pearl beads

Gauge:
27 stitches and 34 rows = 4"/10 cm in stockinette stitch

BACK:

Cast on 92 (94, 100, 106) stitches. Work in stockinette stitch (knit all right-side rows and purl all wrong-side rows), increasing 1 stitch at the beginning and end of every 5 rows 22 (24, 26, 26) times, or until piece measures 13" (14", 15", 16")/33 (35.5, 38, 40) cm—136 (142, 152, 158) stitches. Place stitch markers at the beginning and end of row 72 (76, 80, 88), or 8½" (9", 9½", 10½")/21.5 (23, 24, 27) cm from the cast-on edge.

Bind off 6 stitches at the beginning of every row for 16 (17, 18, 19) rows—40 (40, 44, 44) stitches total. Bind off remaining stitches.

RIGHT FRONT:

For the Right and Left Front pieces, you will work increases and decreases on both the sleeve and the neckline edges at different rates. When the right side of the Right Front is facing up, the sleeve edge is the left edge and the neckline edge is the right edge.

Cast on 12 (13, 13, 14) stitches. Work in stockinette stitch.

Sleeve Edge: Increase 1 stitch at the beginning of every 5 rows until row 112 (118, 125, 137), approximately 13" (14", 15", 16")/ 33 (35.5, 38, 40) cm from cast-on edge. Place a stitch marker at the beginning of row 72 (76, 80, 88), or 8½" (9", 9½", 10½")/21.5 (23, 24, 27) cm from the cast-on edge.

Neckline Edge: *At the same time,* increase 1 stitch at the beginning of every row for 30 (34, 34, 34) rows. Increase 1 stitch at the beginning of every other row for 10 (10, 16, 16) rows. Work even on neckline edge for 8 (8, 8, 8) rows. Decrease 1 stitch every 4 (3, 3, 3) rows until bind off.

To shape shoulder: At row 112 (118, 125, 137), approximately 13" (14", 15", 16")/ 33 (35.5, 38, 40) cm from cast-on edge, start binding off 6 stitches on every sleeve-edge row for 16 (17, 18, 19) rows.

Bind off remaining 6 (6, 6, 6) stitches.

LEFT FRONT:

When the right side of the Left Front is facing up, the sleeve edge is the right edge and the neckline edge is the right edge.

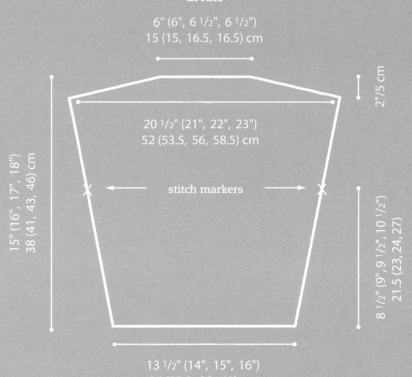

BACK

6" (6", 6 ½", 6 ½")
15 (15, 16.5, 16.5) cm

2"/5 cm

20 ½" (21", 22", 23")
52 (53.5, 56, 58.5) cm

stitch markers

15" (16", 17", 18")
38 (41, 43, 46) cm

8 ½" (9", 9 ½", 10 ½")
21.5 (23, 24, 27)

13 ½" (14", 15", 16")
34 (35.5, 38, 40) cm

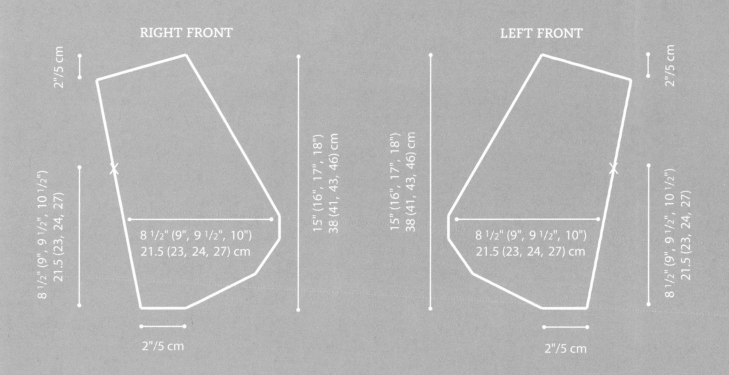

RIGHT FRONT

2"/5 cm

15" (16", 17", 18")
38 (41, 43, 46) cm

8 ½" (9", 9 ½", 10 ½")
21.5 (23, 24, 27)

8 ½" (9", 9 ½", 10")
21.5 (23, 24, 27) cm

2"/5 cm

LEFT FRONT

2"/5 cm

15" (16", 17", 18")
38 (41, 43, 46) cm

8 ½" (9", 9 ½", 10 ½")
21.5 (23, 24, 27)

8 ½" (9", 9 ½", 10")
21.5 (23, 24, 27) cm

2"/5 cm

Cast on 12 (13, 13, 14) stitches. Work in stockinette stitch.

Sleeve Edge: Increase 1 stitch at the beginning of every 5 rows until row 112 (118, 125, 137), approximately 13" (14", 15", 16")/ 33 (35.5, 38, 40) cm from cast-on edge. Place a stitch marker at the beginning of row 72 (76, 80, 88), or 8½" (9", 9½", 10½")/21.5 (23, 24, 27) cm from the cast-on edge.

Neckline Edge: *At the same time,* increase 1 stitch at the beginning of every row for 30 (34, 34, 34) rows. Increase 1 stitch at the beginning of every other row for 10 (10, 16, 16) rows. Work even on neckline edge for 8 (8, 8, 8) rows. Decrease 1 stitch every 4 (3, 3, 3) rows until bind off.

To shape shoulder: at row 112 (118, 125, 137), approximately 13" (14", 15", 16")/ 33 (35.5, 38, 40) cm from cast-on edge, start binding off 6 stitches on every sleeve-edge row for 16 (17, 18, 19) rows.

Bind off remaining 6 (6, 6, 6) stitches.

FINISHING:
Weave in all loose ends with the tapestry needle.

With the tapestry needle and yarn, pin and sew together the shoulder seams using backstitch. Pin and sew together the side seams using backstitch.

Use a sewing pin to mark the center of the back of the neck. To make the lace trim, fold over one end of the lace towards the wrong side approximately ¼"/.6 cm from the edge. Fold again and, using the sewing needle and thread, whipstitch the hem to the wrong side of the lace using very small stitches. Starting at the center of the back of the neck, pin the lace very close to the edge of the top so the right side of the lace is facing outwards and the straight edge of the lace just covers the "bumpy" edges of the knitted piece.

Pin the lace trim all the way around the edges of the front and back of the top until you return to the center of the back of the neck again. Whipstitch the lace trim to the top using very small, barely noticeable stitches. Remove the pins as you go.

Cut the other end of the lace ½"/1 cm past the starting place, fold it over twice towards the wrong side of the lace and whipstitch the hem closed. Whipstitch the two ends of the lace trim together.

Place pins evenly spaced along the lace trim on the front of the top to mark where you would like the freshwater pearl beads to be placed. There should be 6 beads on either side. Sew the beads to the lace edging, removing the pins as you go.

16. bridal stole

With its flowing lace feather and fan stitch in a gorgeous blend of light baby alpaca and rayon, this wrap is fit for a bride. I made it for a friend who was married on a pretty patio at an adorable restaurant in Los Angeles. It looked beautiful over her dress. The ivory color and long rectangular shape make it versatile enough to wear long after the wedding with any color in your wardrobe. Or you can wrap it loosely two or three times around your neck to wear as a scarf.

bridal stole

Experience Level:
Intermediate

Size:
One size fits all

Finished Measurements:
26½" wide × 85" long/67.5 cm × 216 cm

Yarn:
7 skeins Suss Ultrasoft (40% viscose/30% alpaca/20% acrylic 10% nylon; 1.5 ounces/43 grams; 204 yards/188 meters), color Ivory

Notions:
1   size 9 (5.5 mm) circular needles, 24"/61 cm long
tapestry needle

Gauge:
20 stitches and 20 rows = 4"/10 cm in feather and fan pattern

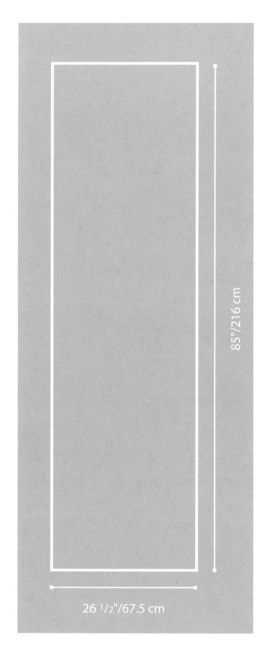

85"/216 cm

26 1/2"/67.5 cm

Cast on 132 stitches. Work four rows in garter stitch (knit all stitches).

Begin working the four-row feather and fan pattern as follows:

Row 1: Knit all stitches.

Row 2: Knit 3, purl all stitches until last 3 stitches, knit 3.

Row 3: Knit 3, * knit 2 together 3 times; (knit 1, yarn over) 6 times; knit2 together 3 times * repeat from * to * until last 3 stitches, knit 3.

Row 4: Knit all stitches.

Continue in this four-row pattern until piece measures approximately 84" or approximately 420 rows, ending with row 4.

Knit 4 rows in garter stitch.

Bind off loosely.

FINISHING:
Weave in all loose ends with the tapestry needle.

17. wedding wrap

The shape and size of this luxurious wrap is very different from the Bridal Stole. It's smaller and more shawl-like, draping straight down from the shoulders into narrow pieces that you can tie softly in front. Champagne-colored silk ribbon threads through the mohair yarn for added texture. It's light enough for even a warm-weather wedding, and you could wear it later over a camisole or tank top and jeans for a romantic picnic or outdoor concert.

wedding wrap

Experience Level:
Intermediate

Size:
One size fits most

Finished Measurements:
Approximately 60" long × 18" wide/152 cm × 46 cm (see diagrams)

Yarn:
3 skeins Suss Candy (35% mohair/30% viscose/20% polyester/10% wool/5% nylon;
1.5 ounces/ 43 grams; 47 yards/43 meters), color Pearl

Notions:
1   pair size 13 (9 mm) needles
1   pair size 7 (4.5 mm) needles
     large tapestry needle
5   yards/5 meters 100% silk ribbon, color Champagne
     sewing pins

Gauge:
12 stitches and 14 rows = 4"/10cm in stockinette stitch with size 13 needles
18 stitches and 22 rows = 4"/10 cm in stockinette stitch with size 7 needles

Cast on 10 stitches with the larger needles. Work in the following pattern for 56 rows, approximately 16"/40.5 cm:

Rows 1 and 3: Knit all stitches, increase 1 stitch at the end of the row.

Row 2: Increase 1 stitch at the beginning of the row, purl all stitches.

Row 4: Purl all stitches.

Repeat Rows 1–4 fourteen times—52 stitches, 56 rows total.

Repeat Rows 1 and 2—54 stitches, 58 rows total.

Work in the following pattern for 56 rows, approximately 32"/81 cm from cast-on edge:

Rows 1 and 3: Knit 2 stitches together, knit all remaining stitches.

Row 2: Purl 2 stitches together, purl all remaining stitches.

Row 4: Purl all stitches.

Repeat Rows 1–4 fourteen times—12 stitches, 114 rows total.

Repeat Rows 1 and 2—10 stitches, 116 rows total.

Bind off loosely.

To make the ties, pick up 13 stitches with the smaller needles along the 10 stitches of the straight narrow edge of the wrap (see diagram 1). You will need to pick up approximately 4 stitches for every 3 stitches worked with the larger needles. Work in stockinette stitch for 14"/35.5 cm. Bind off loosely.

Repeat this process on the other narrow edge of the wrap to make the other tie.

FINISHING:
Weave in all loose ends with the tapestry needle.

Fold the wrap in half to find the center line (see diagram 2) and use two sewing pins to mark the center

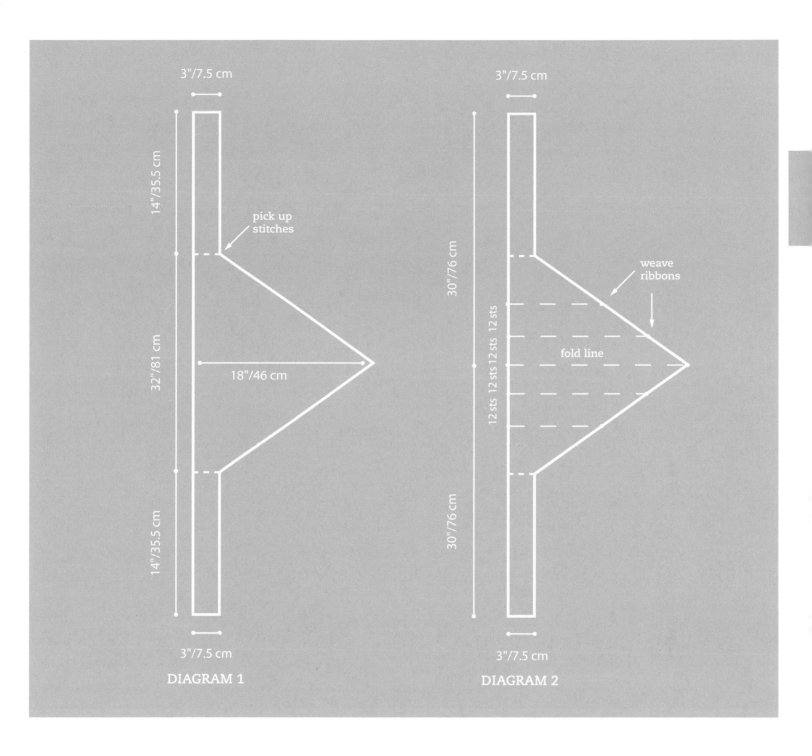

DIAGRAM 1

3"/7.5 cm

14"/35.5 cm

pick up stitches

32"/81 cm

18"/46 cm

14"/35.5 cm

3"/7.5 cm

DIAGRAM 2

3"/7.5 cm

30"/76 cm

weave ribbons

12 sts 12 sts 12 sts 12 sts

fold line

30"/76 cm

3"/7.5 cm

of the top edge of the wrap and the apex of the triangle at the bottom of the wrap. Place additional markers at 12 rows and 24 rows from the center marker in each direction. You will now have 5 markers altogether. Do the same on the bottom edges of the wrap, placing markers 12 and 24 rows from the bottom center marker.

Thread the ribbon through the tapestry needle. Insert the needle and ribbon through the underside of the wrap (the wrong side) at the top center marker about ¼"/1 cm (1 stitch) from the edge. Loop the ribbon around the edge of the wrap and reinsert it through

the same hole leaving a 2½"/6.5 cm tail. Weave the ribbon in and out of the wrap every 3 stitches (approximately 1"/2.5 cm) until you reach the bottom center marker. Make sure you weave along the same row of stitches to keep the ribbons straight. Secure the ribbon to the bottom edge of the wrap using the same method you used at the top edge and cut the ribbon approximately 6"/15 cm from the bottom edge.

Repeat the same process four more times using the other sewing pins as guides for weaving the ribbon.

18. something-blue garter

Wearing a garter on your wedding day is not a Swedish custom, but I know that wearing the color blue symbolizes purity and faithfulness. In the past, brides would add a band of blue around the bottom of a dress. Today, we usually wear our blue on a garter. But this one is too special to toss to a bachelor at your reception—save it for your wedding night and have your new husband remove it. Then you'll have a handmade keepsake.

something-blue garter

Experience Level:
Beginner

Size:
Circumference 14"/35.5 cm

Finished Measurements:
22" wide × 1½" long/56 cm × 4 cm

Yarn:
1 skein Suss Crystal (60% cotton/40% viscose; 1.5 ounces/43 grams; 90 yards/83 meters), color Bleach

Notions:
1   pair size 9 (5.5 mm) circular needles, 24"/61 cm long
    large tapestry needle
    sewing pins
    sewing needle and white thread
    24"/61 cm elastic, ¼"/.6 cm wide (elastic and the decorative notions listed below
    are available at most craft and fabric stores)
    ¼"/.6 cm-wide blue rose trim, 24"/61 cm long
    2"/5 cm-wide crocheted lace trim, 24"/61 cm long
1   yard blue cotton ribbon, ¼"/.6 cm-wide

Gauge:
18 stitches and 22 rows = 4"/10 cm in stockinette stitch

GARTER:

Cast on 100 stitches loosely. Work in stockinette stitch (knit all right-side rows and purl all wrong-side rows) for 1½"/4 cm, or approximately 8 rows.

Bind off loosely.

FINISHING:

Weave in all loose ends with the tapestry needle.

Fold the knitted piece in half lengthwise (with the cast-on and bind-off edges meeting) and use a steam iron to *gently* press the fold into place.

Pin the blue rose trim lengthwise along the center of the bottom half of the knitted piece (see diagram). Cut the excess trim about ¼"/.6 cm longer than the knitted piece. With the sewing needle and thread, whipstitch the blue rose trim to the knitted piece using small, inconspicuous stitches.

Fold over one of the ends of the crocheted lace approximately ½"/1 cm. Fold it over again and pin. With the sewing needle and thread, whipstitch this hem securely to make a finished edge. Repeat for the other end.

Pin the straight edge of the lace to the long edge of the knitted piece right below the blue rose trim, approximately ¼"/.6 cm from the edge. With the sewing needle and thread, whipstitch the lace to the knitted piece using very small stitches.

Fold the piece in half *widthwise* to determine the center and, with the sewing needle and thread, attach the blue ribbon rose to knitted piece on top of the blue rose trim.

Create a channel for the elastic: Fold the knitted piece in half lengthwise and whipstitch the cast-on and bind-off edges closed. Thread the elastic through the channel. Pin one end of the elastic to one end of

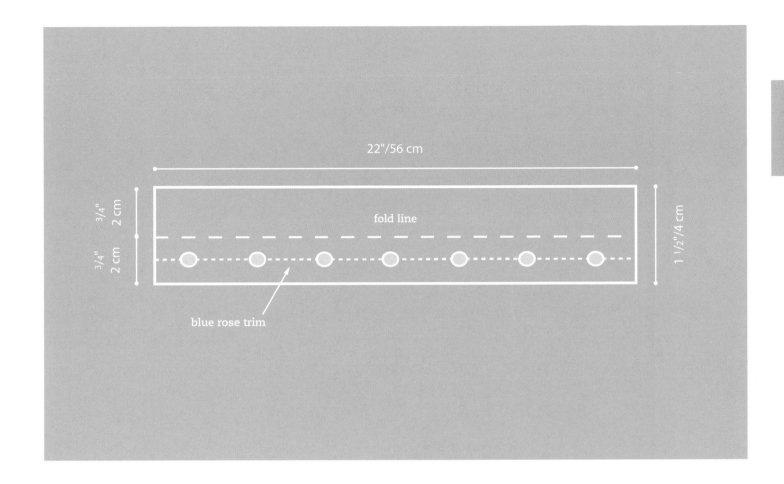

22"/56 cm

3/4"
2 cm
3/4"
2 cm

fold line

blue rose trim

1 1/2"/4 cm

the channel and gather the garter until it measures 12"/30.5 cm. Trim any excess elastic and sew the two ends of the elastic securely together.

Fold the garter so the two ends of the channel meet. Tuck the ends of the blue rose trim into the knitted channel. Pin together the ends of the knitted channel and the crocheted lace trim. With the sewing needle and thread, sew the ends of the channel and the crocheted lace trim together.

Thread the cotton ribbon through the tapestry needle and weave the ribbon through the holes in the crocheted pattern at the bottom edge of the lace trim. Tie the ribbon in a bow and trim the ends about 4"/10 cm from the bow.

19. tasseled silk bridal purse

Exquisite hand-dyed silk yarn and an open knit make this bag a delicate treasure lined in an iridescent silk dupioni. Quartz beads and tassels give it the extra polish a bride wants. The brioche stitch, which creates a ribbed effect, may take a little getting used to at first. Once you get going, this purse will finish up quickly and look as if you spent a lot of time on it.

tasseled silk bridal purse

Experience Level:
Intermediate

Finished measurements of purse:
Approximately 8" × 6"/20 cm × 15 cm

Yarn:
1 skein Suss Silk (100% silk; 1.5 ounces/43 grams; 163 yards/150 meters), color Sand Satin

Notions:
1   pair size 10 (6 mm) needles
     large tapestry needle
     9" × 12"/23 cm × 30 cm piece of 100% silk dupioni fabric, color Dust
     straight pins
     sewing needle and thread in complementary color
1   12"/30.5 cm strand of quartz chip beads (available at most bead stores)
1   size G (4 mm) crochet hook

Gauge:
16 stitches and 20 rows = 4"/10 cm in brioche stitch

PURSE:
Cast on 33 stitches.

Foundation Row (not repeated): With the yarn held in back, slip the first stitch as if to knit (knitwise), [slip 1 yarn over, knit 1], repeat until the end of the row.

Brioche Row 1: With the yarn held in back, slip the first stitch as if to knit (knitwise), [knit 2 together, slip 1 yarn over], repeat until last 2 stitches, knit 2 together, knit 1.

Brioche Row 2: With the yarn held in back, slip the first stitch as if to knit (knitwise), [slip 1 yarn over, knit 2 together], repeat until last 2 stitches, slip one yarn over, knit 1.

Repeat Rows 1 and 2 until piece measures 12"/30 cm, or approximately 60 rows. Bind off loosely.

Special Stitches:

Slip 1 yarn over: Bring working yarn to front between the two needles, slip 1 stitch as if to knit (knitwise),

and then bring the working yarn over the top of the right needle to the back, crossing over the previous (slipped) stitch. This combination "slip 1 yarn over" is counted as one stitch.

Knit 2 together: In brioche stitch, "knit 2 together" means to knit the slipped stitch from the previous row together with the yarn over that went with it. Since the "slip 1 yarn over" from the previous row is counted as one stitch, no stitches have been decreased.

FINISHING:
Weave in all loose ends with the tapestry needle.

Fold the knitted piece in half widthwise with the wrong sides facing each other. Whipstitch the sides together with the tapestry needle and yarn.

Fold the fabric in half as well, with the right sides facing each other. Sew up the sides using the sewing needle and thread, leaving about ½"/1 cm open at the top edge. You may find it helpful to pin the seams first before sewing. Fold over the unseamed top hem twice and

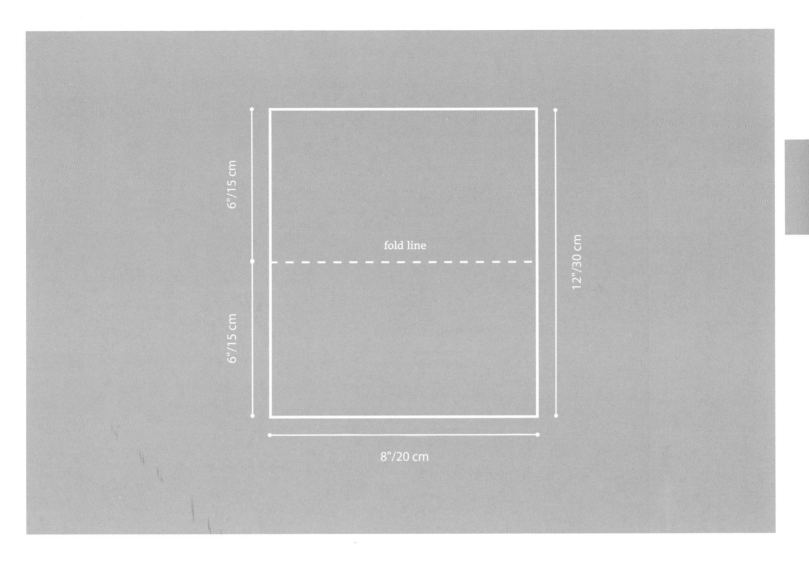

6"/15 cm

fold line

6"/15 cm

12"/30 cm

8"/20 cm

whipstitch it to the wrong side of the lining. Make sure that you keep your stitches small and even since they will be visible on the inside lining of the purse. Do not turn this lining right-side out.

Insert the lining into the knitted purse using the side seams as your placement guides and pin it into place on the top edge of the purse. The hem of the lining should be placed very close to the top edge of the purse, right underneath the cast-on and bind-off rows.

At each of the side seams, insert approximately ½"/1 cm of the quartz chip strand into the space between the lining and the knitted purse and pin each end of the strand into place. Whipstitch the hem of the lining to the knitted purse, removing the pins as you go. Make sure that you attach the ends of the quartz chip strand securely by tacking it to both the lining and the knitted purse with extra stitches.

To make the drawstring tie, work a single chain 30"/76 cm long with the crochet hook and yarn. With the tapestry needle, use a running stitch to weave the crochet chain in and out through the stitches a couple rows below the top outside edge of the purse; each stitch should be about 1"/2.5 cm long. Start and end at the center front of the purse.

To make the tassels, cut the yarn into 14 lengths approximately 4"/10 cm each. Divide the yarn into two groups of 7 lengths each. Fold one of these groups in half to form a loop. Using the crochet hook, pull this loop through one of the ends of the crochet chain, and then pull the ends through this loop and tighten. Repeat for the other end of the crochet chain. Pull the drawstring tight to close the bag.

20. pouf bridal purse

This tiny round pouf of a purse is just big enough to hold a bride's essentials: lipstick, comb, and a mirror. Knit in fuzzy white nylon and decorated with satin roses, it shimmers with reflected light. The drawstring closure is simple to make and, during a long wedding day, easy to carry lightly on the wrist so the bride's hands are free to shake in the receiving line.

pouf bridal purse

Experience Level:
Beginner

Finished Measurements:
 7" wide × 18" long/18 cm × 46 cm
Drawstring casings: 1" wide × 7" long/2.5 cm × 18 cm

Yarn:
2 skeins Suss Icicle (100% nylon; 1 ounce/29 grams; 86 yards/79 meters),
color Snow White

Notions:
1 pair size 6 (4 mm) needles
   large tapestry needle
   sewing pins (optional)
2 white satin ribbon roses, 1½"/4 cm wide (available at most craft stores)
   sewing needle and white thread
2 yards/2 meters white chiffon ribbon, 2"/5 cm wide

Gauge:
22 stitches and 32 rows = 4"/10 cm in stockinette stitch

PURSE:
Cast on 40 stitches. Work in stockinette stitch (knit all right-side rows and purl all wrong-side rows) until piece measures 18"/46 cm, or approximately 144 rows.

Bind off.

To make the casing for the ribbon drawstrings, cast on 6 stitches and work in stockinette stitch until piece measures 7"/18 cm, or approximately 56 rows. Bind off.

Make two.

FINISHING:
Weave in all loose ends with the tapestry needle.

Fold the knitted piece in half so the cast-on and bind-off edges meet. Sew up the two side seams using backstitch (fold with the right sides facing each other) or an invisible vertical join (described below).

To work an invisible vertical join, fold the purse with the wrong sides facing each other and line up all the knit stitches. You may find it helpful to pin the edges together with sewing pins first. Starting with the first stitch at the bottom of the edge on your left, insert the tapestry needle under the horizontal bar between the first and second stitches. Then insert the needle into the corresponding bar on the righthand edge. Draw the pieces together so the two stitch halves resemble one complete knit stitch. Continue in this fashion up the side seam, alternating from the lefthand stitches to the right until you reach the end of the seam.

Using the sewing needle and white thread, attach the satin ribbon roses to the right-side center of one of the drawstring casings. When you attach the casings to the purse, the roses should be centered on the front of the purse.

With the tapestry needle and yarn, attach the casings approximately 2½"/6.5 cm from the top edge of the purse using whipstitch. You may find it helpful to pin the casings to the sides of the purse before attaching them. Leave the casings unclosed at the side seams in order to thread the ribbon drawstrings through the openings.

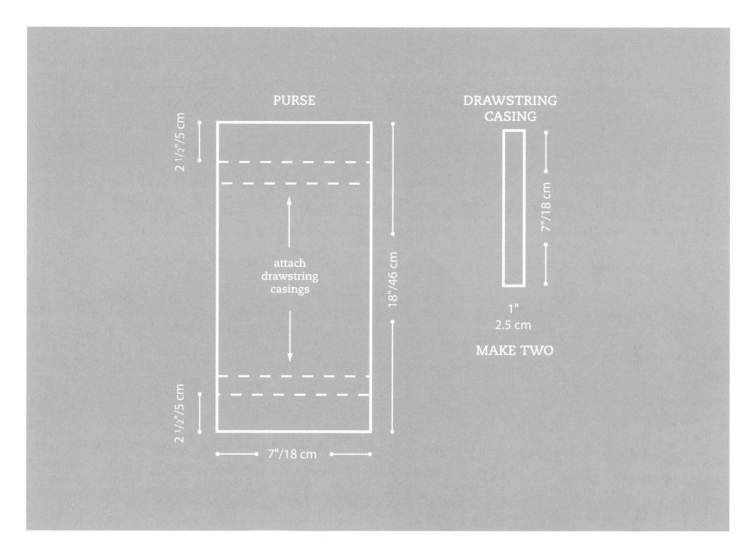

PURSE

2 1/2"/5 cm

attach
drawstring
casings

18"/46 cm

2 1/2"/5 cm

7"/18 cm

DRAWSTRING
CASING

7"/18 cm

1"
2.5 cm

MAKE TWO

To make the drawstrings, cut the ribbon into two lengths 1 yard/1 meter each. Thread the tapestry needle with one end of ribbon and work the needle and ribbon through one of the casings. In a similar manner, work the other ribbon through the casing on the other side of the purse. Tie the ends of the two ribbons together in small knots and cut the ribbon close to the knots.

21. fingerless long gloves

Remember those long, long gloves that all the movie stars from the 1930s wore with their slinky bias-cut satin gowns? We don't have much occasion to wear such formal attire today, so going all out for your wedding is such fun. These gloves are knit in ivory alpaca with a very narrow rib stitch. You seam them in an open stitch that makes them look a bit lacy. The little tie on top is romantic and sweet. For after wedding wear, you could make the gloves in a dark color to wear with jeans and a tank top.

fingerless long gloves

Experience Level:
Intermediate

Size:
One size fits most

Finished Measurements:
Each glove measures approximately 7½" × 21"/19 cm × 53.5 cm (see diagram)

Yarn:
4 skeins Suss Alpaca (100% alpaca; 2 ounces/57 grams; 163 yards/150 meters),
color Natural

Notions:
1   pair size 6 (4 mm) needles
    large tapestry needle
1   size G (4 mm) crochet hook

Gauge:
32 stitches and 30 rows = 4"/10 cm in one-by-one rib stitch

GLOVES:

Cast on 52 stitches loosely. Work in one-by-one rib stitch (knit 1 stitch, purl 1 stitch, and repeat until the end of the row) for 2"/5 cm.

THUMBHOLE SHAPING:

On the next row, work 26 stitches in rib pattern. Start a new ball of yarn and work the next 26 stitches in rib pattern on the same needles using this new ball. Turn and continue to work in rib pattern on the two balls separately for 10 additional rows. This will create the slit for the thumbhole.

When you have completed 10 rows, work across all 52 stitches using the original ball of yarn. Cut the tail of the second ball.

Work even in rib pattern until piece measures 15"/38 cm from cast-on edge.

Increase one stitch at the beginning of the next two rows while maintaining the rib pattern—54 stitches.

Work even in rib pattern until piece measures 17"/43 cm and increase 1 stitch at the beginning of the next two rows—56 stitches. Work even until piece measures 19"/48 cm and increase one stitch at the beginning

of the next two rows—58 stitches total.

Work even in rib pattern until piece measures 21"/53.5 cm. Bind off in rib pattern.

Make two gloves.

FINISHING:

Weave in all loose ends with the tapestry needle.

With the tapestry needle and two strands of yarn, whipstitch the gloves together using stitches approximately ½"/1 cm stitches long. When you wear the gloves, these stitches will be showing on the outside. Repeat this process for the second glove.

With the crochet hook and yarn, work a single crochet chain approximately 15"/38 cm long, or whatever length you desire. Thread this chain through the tapestry needle. Beginning at the side seam approximately 2"/5 cm from the bind-off edge, insert the needle and thread through the right side of the glove and work a running stitch loosely around the circumference of the entire glove. Make sure you leave a short tail. After you've worked around to the beginning, tie the two ends of the crochet chain into a bow. Repeat for the second glove.

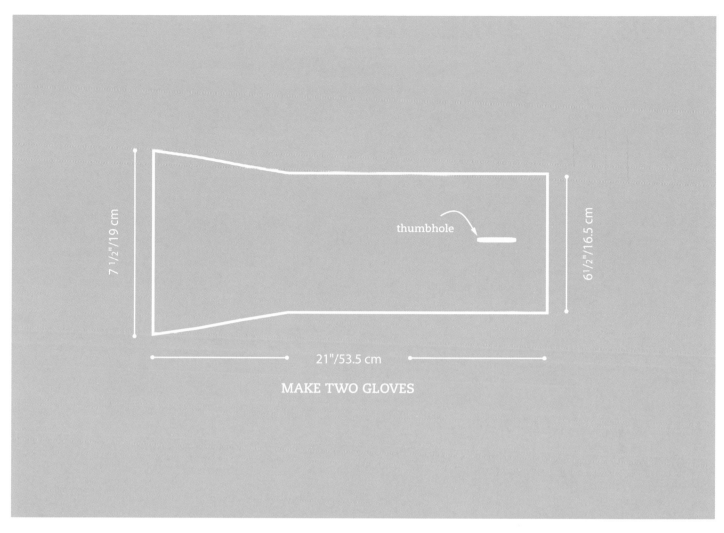

7 ¹/₂"/19 cm

6¹/₂"/16.5 cm

thumbhole

21"/53.5 cm

MAKE TWO GLOVES

22. jewel keeper

For the bride's diamonds and pearls, this special little storage bag is perfect. I decorated it with sequins and finished it off with handpainted silk ribbon. Although it's easy to knit, the end result looks as if you spent hours on it. You could create a family tradition by passing down an heirloom ring in this delicate container.

jewel keeper

Experience Level:
Beginner

Finished Measurements:
5" wide × 14" long/13 cm × 35.5 cm

Yarn:
1 skein Suss Feather (100% polyamide; 2.5 ounces/71 grams; 145 yards/134 meters), color Dove

Notions:
- 1 pair size 6 (4 mm) needles large tapestry needle
- 1 crochet hook size G (4 mm)
- 8 white iridescent sequins, ¼" wide sewing needle and thread in complementary color
- 1 ½ yards/1.5 meters variegated blue silk ribbon, 1"/2.5 cm wide

Gauge:
20 stitches and 28 rows = 4"/10 cm in stockinette stitch

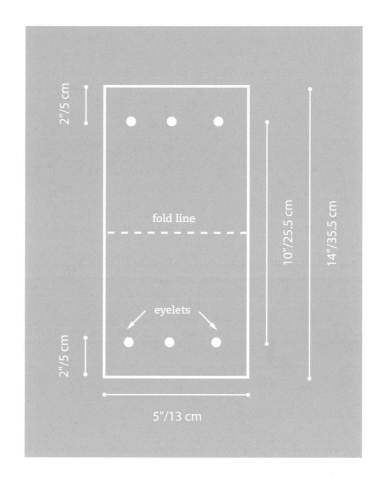

Cast on 26 stitches. Work in stockinette stitch (knit all right-side rows and purl all wrong-side rows) until piece measures 2"/5 cm, or approximately 14 rows, ending with a wrong-side row.

Work eyelet row as follows:

Knit 4 stitches, yarn over, knit 2 together, [knit 6, yarn over, knit 2 together] twice, knit 4.

Continue in stockinette until piece measures 12"/30.5 cm from cast-on edge, or approximately 84 rows total, ending with a wrong-side row. Work another eyelet row.

Work even until piece measures 14"/35.5 cm, or approximately 100 rows total.

Bind off loosely.

FINISHING:
Weave in all loose ends with the tapestry needle.

With the wrong sides facing each other, fold the knitted piece in half so the cast-on and bind-off edges meet and the eyelet rows are lined up. With the crochet hook, use single crochet to attach the side seams together.

With the sewing needle and thread, attach the sequins to one side of the bag (the front) in a random fashion wherever you would like to see a little sparkle.

Thread the silk ribbon through the tapestry needle and, starting at one of the eyelet holes nearest to one of the side seams, thread the ribbon in and out of the eyelet holes until you work around to the starting point again. Pull the ribbon tight and tie it in a bow. Tie small knots in the ribbon wherever you'd like the ribbon to end and cut each end of the ribbon very closely to these knots.

3

So often brides spend a lot of time picking out their wedding-day clothes and accessories but then forget about the "ever after." That's where this section comes in handy. First are patterns for the long-awaited wedding night. You can be sexy *and* comfortable in my Wedding Night Robe, Sexy Nightie, or Angora Camisole and Shorts. The nightgown, for instance, is knit in stockinette on circular needles with a yarn called Ultrasoft because it contains baby alpaca. A chocolate-brown ribbon circles an empire waist. ✳ I've designed projects like the Soft Monogrammed Throw and cabled Vacation Scarves for traveling to a honeymoon destination. The throw is warm and light without being scratchy. ✳ Once you're there, slip into the Soft Striped Bikini or Wraparound Skirt, and you'll feel carefree and relaxed. The All-Season Sweater is a great resort piece knit in incredibly soft white yarn on big needles. ✳ Try to finish anything you want to wear before your wedding. On this one occasion, even I think you should leave your knitting behind and be ready for having fun with your new husband. After all, it's your honeymoon!

23. wedding night robe

For your wedding night, you want to wear something that makes you feel like a princess, which is why a beautiful Swedish cake called a Princess Torte inspired this delicious robe. The cake is green marzipan with ivory and baby-pink flowers. I adapted those colors, so the robe is made in ivory with pink and aqua accents: tiny embroidered flowers and vines are embroidered around the neckline and cuffs. After all, it's worth putting a bit of extra time into a garment that will help you have a night to remember. A short wrap style with wide sleeves is both sexy and simple worn over a little pink nightie. Luscious!

wedding night robe

Experience Level:
Advanced

Size:
One size
Chest: 36"/91 cm
Length: 35"/89 cm

Finished Measurements:
Back: 28" wide × 35" long/71 cm × 89 cm
Right and Left Front: 16" wide × 35" long/40.5 cm × 89 cm

Yarn:
A: 13 skeins Suss Snuggle (60% cotton/40% acrylic; 2 ounces/57 grams; 126 yards/116 meters), color Naturale
B: 1 skein Suss Fishnet (53% acrylic/30% nylon/17% alpaca; 1.5 ounces/43 grams; 285 yards/263 meters), color Aqua
C: 1 skein Suss Melange (50% polyamide, 30% acrylic, 20% alpaca); 1.5 ounces/43 grams; 153 yards/141 meters), color Ice Pink

Notions:
1   pair size 9 (5.5 mm) circular needles, 24"/61 cm long
1   pair size 7 (4.5 mm) needles
1   knitting row counter (recommended)
6   stitch markers
    large tapestry needle
    sewing pins
1   size G (4 mm) crochet hook

Gauge:
17 stitches and 22 rows = 4"/10 cm in stockinette stitch with size 9 needles
28 stitches and 28 rows = 4"/10 cm in one-by-one rib stitch with size 7 needles

BACK:
Cast on 120 stitches with size 9 needles. Work in stockinette stitch (knit all right-side rows and purl all wrong-side rows) until piece measures 23"/58.5 cm long, or 126 rows, ending with a wrong-side row. Place stitch markers at the beginning and end of this row.

To shape armholes, decrease one stitch at the beginning and end of every other row for 6 rows—114 stitches total. Work even until pieces measures 33"/84 cm from cast-on edge or 184 rows, ending with a wrong-side row.

Bind off 8 stitches at the beginning of the next 8 rows—50 stitches total. Bind off 9 stitches at the beginning of the next 2 rows—32 stitches total.

Bind off.

SLEEVES:
Cast on 90 stitches with size 9 needles. Work in stockinette increasing 1 stitch at the beginning and the end of every 9 rows for 54 rows—102 stitches total. Bind off 4 stitches at the beginning of every row for 8 rows—70 stitches total. Bind off.

Make two.

LEFT FRONT:
Cast on 68 stitches with size 9 needles. Work in stockinette until piece measures 17½"/44.5 cm from cast-on edge, or 96 rows, ending with a wrong-side row. Place a stitch marker at the beginning of this wrong-side row.

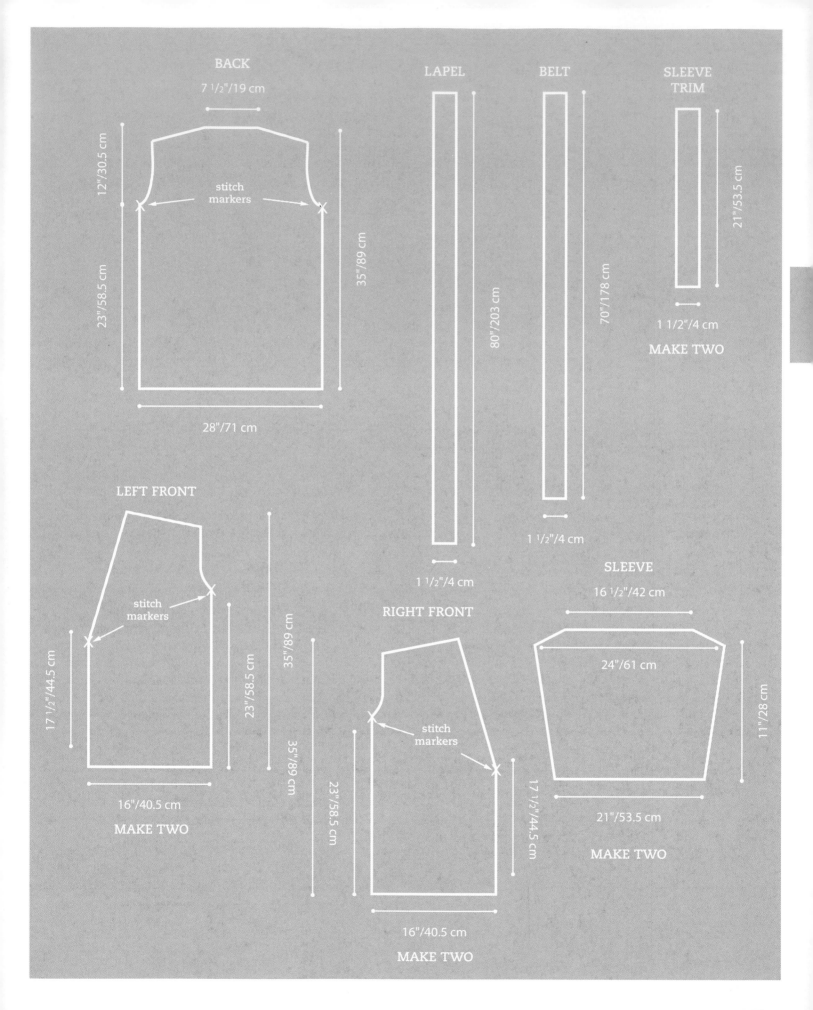

BACK

7 1/2"/19 cm

12"/30.5 cm

stitch markers

23"/58.5 cm

35"/89 cm

28"/71 cm

LAPEL

80"/203 cm

1 1/2"/4 cm

BELT

70"/178 cm

1 1/2"/4 cm

SLEEVE TRIM

21"/53.5 cm

1 1/2"/4 cm

MAKE TWO

LEFT FRONT

stitch markers

17 1/2"/44.5 cm

23"/58.5 cm

35"/89 cm

16"/40.5 cm

MAKE TWO

RIGHT FRONT

35"/89 cm

23"/58.5 cm

stitch markers

16"/40.5 cm

MAKE TWO

SLEEVE

16 1/2"/42 cm

24"/61 cm

11"/28 cm

17 1/2"/44.5 cm

21"/53.5 cm

MAKE TWO

Start shaping neckline by decreasing 1 stitch every 4 rows along the neckline edge (the same edge as the stitch marker) until bind off. Work until piece measures 23"/58.5 cm, or 126 rows, from cast-on edge ending with a wrong-side row. Place stitch marker at the end of this wrong-side row.

To shape armhole, decrease 1 stitch at the beginning of every right-side row for 6 rows while maintaining decrease pattern on neckline edge. Work even on armhole edge until piece measures 33"/84 cm from the cast-on edge, or 184 rows. Bind off 8 stitches at the beginning of every right-side row for the next 9 rows.

Bind off remaining 9 stitches.

RIGHT FRONT:

Cast on 68 stitches with size 9 needles. Work in stockinette until piece measures 17½"/44.5 cm from cast-on edge, or 96 rows, ending with a wrong-side row. Place a stitch marker at the end of this wrong-side row.

Start shaping neckline by decreasing 1 stitch every 4 rows along the neckline edge (the same edge as the stitch marker) until bind off. Work until piece measures 23"/58.5 cm, or 126 rows, from cast-on edge ending with a wrong-side row. Place stitch marker at the beginning of this wrong-side row.

To shape armhole, decrease 1 stitch at the beginning of every wrong-side row for 6 rows while maintaining decrease pattern on neckline edge. Work even on armhole edge until piece measures 33"/84 cm from the cast-on edge, or 184 rows. Bind off 8 stitches at the beginning of every wrong-side row for the next 9 rows.

Bind off remaining 9 stitches.

BELT:

Cast on 10 stitches with size 7 needles.

Work in a one-by-one rib stitch (knit 1 stitch, purl 1 stitch, and repeat until the end of the row) until belt measures 70"/178 cm, or whatever length you choose.

Bind off.

SLEEVE TRIM:

Cast on 10 stitches with size 7 needles. Work in a one-by-one rib stitch until trim measures 21"/53.5 cm. Bind off.

Make two.

LAPEL:

Cast on 10 stitches with size 7 needles. Work in a one-by-one rib stitch until lapel measures 80"/203 cm.

Bind off.

FINISHING:

Weave in all loose ends with the tapestry needle.

Pin together the shoulder seams and, with the tapestry needle and yarn A, sew the shoulder seams using backstitch. Pin the side seams together making sure you line up the stitch markers as your guides. Sew the side seams using backstitch, starting at the bottom hem and stopping at the stitch markers.

Copy the floral embroidery pattern provided onto several pieces of tracing paper. Pin the pieces of paper to the Lapel and Sleeve Trim pieces matching up the start and end points of the continuous vine design. The length of the pattern will not match precisely with the length of the Lapel and Sleeve Trim. Simply end the pattern wherever is convenient and trim the excess tracing paper.

With the tapestry needle and yarn B, embroider the leaves and vines first using chain stitch for the vines and lazy daisy stitch for the leaves. With the tapestry needle and yarn C, embroider the star flowers in straight stitch. When you are done embroidering, simply tear away the tracing paper. Any leftover scraps can be removed with tweezers.

Pin the Lapel in a continuous line starting at the bottom of the Left Front, around the collar and down the edge of the Right Front. Whipstitch the lapel to the edges with the tapestry needle and yarn A. In a similar fashion, pin and whipstitch the Sleeve Trim to the long (21"/53.5 cm) edge of the Sleeves.

Close the sleeve seams with the tapestry needle and yarn A. Pin and sew the sleeves into the armholes.

To make the Belt loops, use the crochet hook and yarn A to make two chains approximately 3"/8 cm long and, with the tapestry needle and yarn, attach them securely to the side seams so the top of the loop lies approximately 3"/8 cm below the bottom of the armhole. You may want to try on the garment first and mark where you would like the Belt to be placed.

EMBROIDERY PATTERN AND YARN GUIDE

▬ = yarn B (chain stitch)

⬭ = yarn B (lazy daisy stitch)

▬ = yarn C (straight stitch)

24. sexy nightie

After the wedding dress, brides probably care most about what they'll wear on their wedding night. This nightgown is unique and sensual, yet comfortable, in a yarn appropriately called Ultrasoft. Knit in stockinette on circular needles, the nightie has a chocolate-brown ribbon around an empire waist and hand-crocheted butterflies in salmon, brown, and green.

sexy nightie

Experience Level:
Intermediate

Sizes:
Small (medium, large, extra large)

Finished Measurements:
Chest: 30" (32", 34", 36")/76 (81, 86, 91) cm
Length: 30" (31", 32", 33")/76 (79, 81, 84) cm

Yarn:
4 skeins Suss Ultrasoft (40% viscose/30% alpaca/20% acrylic/10% nylon; 1.5 ounces/
43 grams; 204 yards/188 meters), color Bone

Notions:
- 1 pair size 9 (5.5 mm) circular needles, 24"/61 cm long
- 1 knitting row counter
- 1 stitch holder
  large tapestry needle
  sewing pins
- 2 yards/2 meters rayon tape ribbon, ½"/1 cm wide, color Chocolate
- 4 hand-crocheted butterflies, color Salmon/Chocolate/Green
  (available at www.sussdesign.com)
  sewing needle and thread in complementary color
- 1 size G (4 mm) crochet hook

Gauge:
20 stitches and 25 rows = 4"/10 cm in stockinette stitch

FRONT:

Cast on 85 (90, 95, 100) stitches. Work in stockinette stitch (knit all right-side rows and purl all wrong-side rows), casting on 4 stitches at the beginning of every row for 4 rows—101 (106, 111, 116) stitches total. Cast on 5 stitches to the beginning of every row for 4 rows—121 (126, 131, 136) stitches total.

Decrease one stitch at the beginning and end of every 6 (6, 6, 6) rows 17 (20, 22, 21) times—87 (86, 87, 94) stitches total. Decrease one stitch at the beginning and end of every 4 (4, 4, 8) rows 6 (3, 1, 2) times, ending with a wrong-side row—75 (80, 85, 90) stitches total. At the same time, work an eyelet row on the right-side row 18" (19", 20", 21")/46 (48, 51, 53) cm from the cast-on edge.

Eyelet Row: Knit 6 stitches, * yarn over, knit 2 together knit 6 stitches *; repeat from * to * until end of row.

To shape armholes, decrease 1 stitch on the beginning and end of every row for 8 (8, 10, 10) rows—59 (64, 65, 70) stitches total. Decrease 1 stitch at the beginning and end of every other row for 14 (14, 14, 16) rows—45 (50, 51, 54) stitches total. On the next row, work for 17 (20, 20, 22) stitches, bind off 11 (10, 11, 10) stitches, and place remaining 17 (20, 20, 22) stitches on stitch holder.

Join yarn at needle and decrease 1 stitch at the beginning of every wrong-side row and the end of every right-side row for 7 (8, 8, 9) rows. Decrease 1 stitch at the beginning of every wrong-side row for 8 (10, 10, 12) rows. Work even until strap measures 5½" (5½", 6", 6")/14 (14, 15, 15) cm from join.

Work the stitches from the stitch holder. Reverse the shaping to make the other strap.

Bind off loosely.

BACK:

Work as for Front until armholes (including eyelet row). To shape armholes, decrease 1 stitch on the beginning

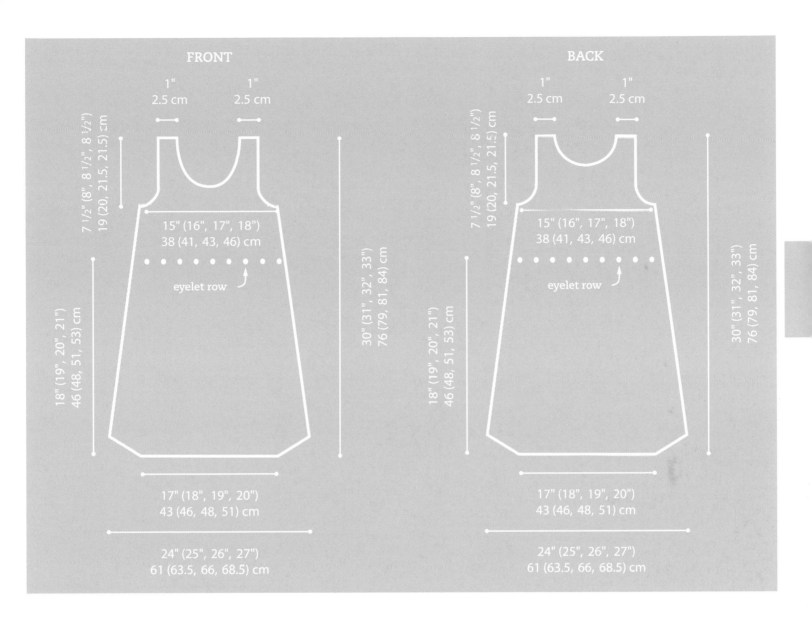

FRONT

1"
2.5 cm

1"
2.5 cm

7 1/2" (8", 8 1/2", 8 1/2") 19 (20, 21.5, 21.5) cm

15" (16", 17", 18")
38 (41, 43, 46) cm

eyelet row

30" (31", 32", 33")
76 (79, 81, 84) cm

18" (19", 20", 21")
46 (48, 51, 53) cm

17" (18", 19", 20")
43 (46, 48, 51) cm

24" (25", 26", 27")
61 (63.5, 66, 68.5) cm

BACK

1"
2.5 cm

1"
2.5 cm

7 1/2" (8", 8 1/2", 8 1/2") 19 (20, 21.5, 21.5) cm

15" (16", 17", 18")
38 (41, 43, 46) cm

eyelet row

30" (31", 32", 33")
76 (79, 81, 84) cm

18" (19", 20", 21")
46 (48, 51, 53) cm

17" (18", 19", 20")
43 (46, 48, 51) cm

24" (25", 26", 27")
61 (63.5, 66, 68.5) cm

and end of every row for 8 (8, 10, 10) rows—59 (64, 65, 70) stitches total. Decrease 1 stitch at the beginning and end of every other row for 14 (14, 14, 16) rows—45 (50, 51, 54) stitches total. Work even for 8 rows. On the next row, work for 17 (20, 20, 22) stitches, bind off 11 (10, 11, 10) stitches, and place remaining 17 (20, 20, 22) stitches on stitch holder.

Join yarn at needle and decrease 1 stitch at the beginning of every wrong-side row and the end of every right-side row for 7 (8, 8, 9) rows. Decrease 1 stitch at the beginning of every wrong-side row for 8 (10, 10, 12) rows. Work even until strap measures 4" (4", 4½", 4½")/10 (10, 11, 11) cm from join.

Work the stitches from the stitch holder. Reverse the shaping to form the other strap.

FINISHING:

Weave in all loose ends with the tapestry needle.

Pin together the shoulder straps and, with the tapestry needle and yarn, sew the shoulder straps using backstitch. Pin the side seams and sew them together using backstitch.

Use four sewing pins to mark the places where you would like to attach the crocheted butterflies. The butterflies should be evenly spaced across the bottom edge of the Front piece. With the sewing needle and thread, whipstitch the crocheted butterflies to the Front.

Thread the tapestry needle with the rayon tape ribbon and, starting in the center of the Front, weave the ribbon in and out of the eyelet holes all the way around the nightie. Tie the ribbon in a bow and trim to desired length.

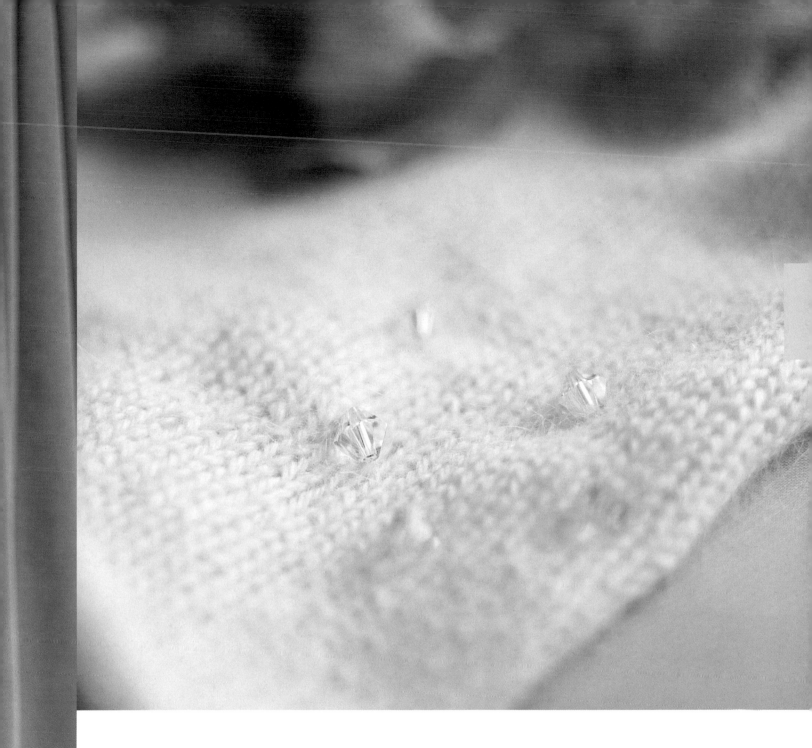

25. angora camisole and shorts set

If you're more of a sporty-type bride, an alternative to the Sexy Nightie for your wedding night is this camisole with boy shorts. The slightly rolled edges and the cut of the bottoms are flattering, and its organza ribbon bows and Austrian crystal trim make it wedding-night worthy. You use tiny size 4 needles, which makes a very finely knit, delicate fabric. After your honeymoon, try the top by itself over jeans.

angora camisole and shorts set

Experience Level:
Intermediate

Sizes:
Small (medium, large, extra-large)

Finished Measurements:
Camisole Chest: 29" (31", 33", 35")/74 (79, 84, 89) cm
Camisole Length: 19" (20", 21", 22")/48 (51, 53, 56) cm
Shorts Waist: 40" (42", 44", 46")/101.5 (106.5, 112, 117) cm
Shorts Length: 10½" (11", 11½", 12")/27 (28, 29, 30.5) cm

Yarn:
3 (3, 4, 4) skeins Suss Angora (70% angora/30% nylon; 1.5 ounces/43 grams; 246 yards/
227 meters), color Ivory

Notions:
1   pair size 4 (3.5 mm) circular needles, 24"/61 cm long
1   stitch holder
1   knitting row counter
    tapestry needle
    sewing pins
    4.5 yards/4 meters silk ribbon, 3/8"/1 cm wide, color Mint Berry
    sewing needle and ivory-colored thread
10 clear 6 mm Austrian crystal beads

Gauge:
28 stitches and 36 rows = 4"/10 cm in stockinette stitch

CAMISOLE BACK:

Cast on 102 (108, 116, 122) stitches. Work in stockinette stitch (knit all right-side rows and purl all wrong-side rows) until piece measures 17¼" (18¼", 18¾", 19¾")/44 (46, 48, 50) cm, or approximately 156 (164, 170, 178) rows, ending with a wrong-side row.

Bind off.

CAMISOLE FRONT:

Cast on 102 (108, 116, 122) stitches. Work in stockinette stitch until piece measures 16½" (17½", 18", 19")/42 (44.5, 46, 48.5) cm, or approximately 148 (158, 162, 170) rows, ending with a wrong-side row.

Work 51 (54, 58, 61) stitches and place remaining 51 (54, 58, 61) stitches on a stitch holder. Decrease 1 stitch at the beginning and end of every row for 23 (24, 26, 28) rows. Bind off the remaining 5 (6, 6, 5) stitches.

Work the stitches from the stitch holder, decreasing 1 stitch at the beginning and end of every row for 23 (24, 26, 28) rows. Bind off the remaining 5 (6, 6, 5) stitches.

LEFT SHORTS:

Cast on 154 (162, 168, 176) stitches. Work in stockinette increasing 1 stitch at the beginning and end of every other row 5 (6, 6, 7) times—164 (174, 180, 190) stitches, 10 (12, 12, 14) rows. Bind off 10 stitches at the beginning of the next 2 rows.

From this point on, you will be decreasing at one continuous rate on the right edge (back seam) and at three different rates on the left edge (front seam). The left and right edges refer to placement of the edges when the right side (knit side) of the piece is facing you.

On the right edge, decrease 1 stitch every 10 rows until bind off.

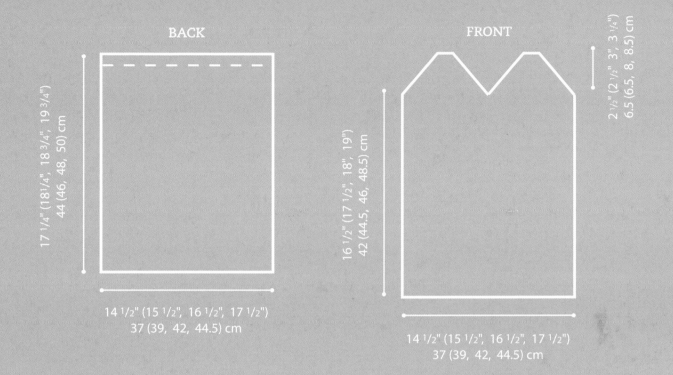

BACK

FRONT

17 ¹/₄" (18¹/₄", 18 ³/₄", 19 ³/₄")
44 (46, 48, 50) cm

14 ¹/₂" (15 ¹/₂", 16 ¹/₂", 17 ¹/₂")
37 (39, 42, 44.5) cm

16 ¹/₂" (17 ¹/₂", 18", 19")
42 (44.5, 46, 48.5) cm

2 ¹/₂" (2 ¹/₂" 3", 3 ¹/₄")
6.5 (6.5, 8, 8.5) cm

14 ¹/₂" (15 ¹/₂", 16 ¹/₂", 17 ¹/₂")
37 (39, 42, 44.5) cm

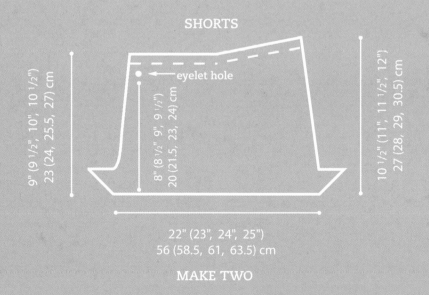

SHORTS

eyelet hole

9" (9 ¹/₂" 10", 10 ¹/₂")
23 (24, 25.5, 27) cm

8" (8 ¹/₂" 9" 9 ¹/₂")
20 (21.5, 23, 24) cm

10 ¹/₂" (11", 11 ¹/₂", 12")
27 (28, 29, 30.5) cm

22" (23", 24", 25")
56 (58.5, 61, 63.5) cm

MAKE TWO

On the left edge, decrease 1 stitch every other row 8 times and then decrease 1 stitch every 10 rows 4 (4, 5, 5) times. *At the same time,* on the right-side row 8" (8½", 9", 9½")/20 (21.5, 23, 24) cm from the cast-on edge, work an eyelet row as follows: knit 6 stitches, yarn over, knit 2 together, and knit until the end of the row. Work even until piece measures 9" (9½", 10", 10½")/23 (24, 25.5, 27) cm from cast-on edge. Bind off 58 (61, 65, 68) stitches. Bind off 7 stitches at the beginning of every other row 7 times.

Bind off remaining stitches.

RIGHT SHORTS:
Work as for Left Shorts, but reverse shaping.

FINISHING:
Weave in all loose ends with the tapestry needle.

Fold over the bind-off edge of the Camisole Back ¾"/2 cm towards the wrong side. Steam *lightly* (this is angora!) and pin. With the tapestry needle and yarn, whipstitch the hem to the wrong side of the Camisole Back.

Place the Camisole Front and Back together with the right sides facing and pin the side seams together. With the tapestry needle and yarn, start where the Camisole Front meets the top edge of the Camisole Back and use backstitch to sew up the side seams with a seam allowance of about 1/8"/0.3 cm. Use this seam allowance for all remaining seams as well. At the bottom of the side seams, tack the cast-on edges to the outside of the side seams about ½"/1 cm from the bottom to reinforce the rolled bottom edges.

To make the front straps, cut the silk ribbon into 2 lengths each 20"/51 cm long. Fold over one end of the ribbon ¼"/1 cm and pin this folded portion to the wrong side of the left top point, approximately ¾"/2 cm from the top. With the sewing needle and thread, tack down this end of the ribbon securely with very small stitches,

which should be nearly invisible from the right side. Repeat this process to attach the other 20"/51 cm length to the top right point of the Camisole Front.

To make the back straps, cut the silk ribbon into 2 lengths each 24"/61 cm long. To mark the place where you will attach the two back straps, place sewing pins on the top hem of the Camisole Back approximately 5" (5", 5½", 6") from the two side seams. You may find it helpful to try on the camisole first to mark the right spots to ensure a proper fit. Attach the ribbon ends as you did for the front straps. Tie small knots at the ends of the front and back ribbon straps and trim the ribbons very close to these knots.

Place the two Shorts pieces together with the right sides facing each other. With the tapestry needle and yarn, sew up the inseams and the front and back seams using backstitch. *Do not* turn the shorts right side out. Fold over the bind-off edges (waist) of the Shorts ¾"/2 cm towards the wrong side. Steam *lightly* and pin. With the tapestry needle and yarn, whipstitch this channel to the wrong side of the waist of the Shorts. Turn the Shorts right side out.

Cut the silk ribbon into a piece about 56"/142 cm long (or as long as you would like the ribbon belt to be) and tie a small knot at one end. Thread this ribbon through one of the eyelet holes in the channel at the waist and work it around the channel and out the other eyelet hole. Make another small knot at the other end of the ribbon.

With the sewing needle and thread, sew 5 of the Austrian crystals beads to the Camisole Front in a random pattern about 3"/8 cm from the bottom and 3"/8 cm from the left side seam. Lay the Shorts flat with the front side facing up and the ribbon tie in the center. Place pins to mark where you would like to attach the crystals and, with the sewing needle and thread, sew 5 of the Austrian crystals to the front of the Shorts. See the photograph for placement suggestions for the crystals, but feel free to try any pattern you like.

26. soft monogrammed throw

Honey-colored yarn is just right for a honeymoon gift. Knit in a wide rib stitch, the throw has fringe and the new couple's monogram embroidered in a corner. You can roll it up into a case like a yoga mat for easy traveling or to use as a pillow—and it's the perfect size to cover a couple on an airplane or anywhere else they may want to snuggle up together.

soft monogrammed throw

Experience Level:
Beginner

Finished Measurements:
52" wide × 60" long/132 cm × 152.5 cm

Yarns:
A: 28 skeins Suss Coolaid (85% acrylic/15% wool;2 ounces/57 grams; 90 yards/
83 meters), color Honey
B: 1 skein Suss Coolaid (85% acrylic/15% wool; 2 ounces/57 grams; 90 yards/
83 meters), color Chocolate

Notions:
  1   pair size 11 (8 mm) circular needles, 47"/119 cm long
      large tapestry needle
  1   size G (4 mm) crochet hook
      tracing paper
      straight pins

Gauge:
12 stitches and 14 rows = 4"/10 cm in three-by-three rib stitch

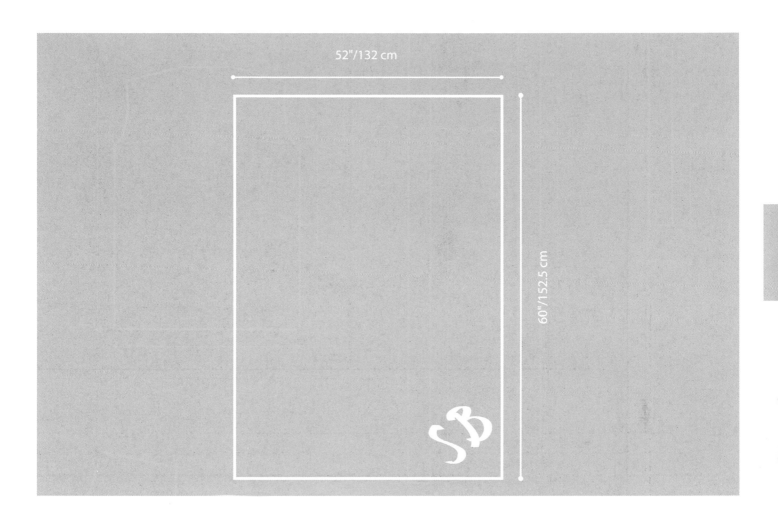

52"/132 cm

60"/152.5 cm

TRAVEL THROW:

Cast on 156 stitches with two strands of yarn A held together. Work in three-by-three rib stitch (knit 3 stitches, purl 3 stitches, and repeat until the end of the row) until piece measures 60"/152.5 cm, or approximately 210 rows.

Bind off in rib pattern.

FINISHING:

Weave in all loose ends with the tapestry needle.

With the crochet hook and two strands of yarn A held together, work a single crochet stitch around all four sides of the throw.

With two strands of yarn B, embroider the initials of the bride and groom in one of the corners of the throw using chain stitch. You can draw your own alphabet or find an alphabet from a book. Copy the letters onto a piece of tracing paper, pin the paper to the corner of the blanket,

and stitch over the outlines of the letters. When you are done embroidering, simply tear away the tracing paper. Any leftover scraps can be removed with tweezers.

Cut yarn A into 128 lengths 18"/46 cm each. Divide these lengths into four groups of 32 each. Fold one of these groups in half to form a loop. Using the crochet hook, pull this loop through one of the corners of the blanket, pull the ends through this loop, and tighten. Repeat this process to add fringe to all the corners of the blanket.

27. soft striped bikini

I like to design bikinis with adjustable straps for avoiding tan lines. Knitted bikinis without Lycra aren't really for swimming—they're for sunbathing. This version has beautiful colors—sky blue paired with an ivory. The skinny stripe pattern is easy to wear. Its crocheted edges help keep its shape, while the wooden beads add something unusual.

soft striped bikini

Experience Level:
Advanced

Size:
One size, fits chest 36"/91 cm

Finished Measurements:
Bottom: Approximately 12" wide × 20" long/30.5 × 51 cm (see diagram)
Top: approximately 7" wide × 8" long/18 × 20 cm each side (see diagram)

Yarns:
A: 1 skein Suss Snuggle (60% cotton/40% acrylic; 2 ounces/57 grams; 126 yards/ 116 meters), color Naturale
B: 1 skein Suss Snuggle (60% cotton/40% acrylic; 2 ounces/57 grams; 126 yards/ 116 meters), color Sky Blue

Notions:
1 pair size 6 (4 mm) needles
   large tapestry needle
   sewing pins
1 size E (3.5 mm) crochet hook
   sewing needle and thread in complementary color
18 10 mm wooden beads

Gauge:
20 stitches and 28 rows = 4"/10 cm in stockinette stitch

BOTTOM:

Cast on 60 stitches with yarn A. To make the casing, work even in stockinette stitch (knit all right-side rows and purl all wrong-side rows) for 2 rows. Change to yarn B and work for 2 rows. Work even, alternating colors every 2 rows, until piece measures 2"/5 cm, or 14 rows, ending with a wrong side row. Continue switching colors every 2 rows throughout the entire piece. Since the stripes are so small, carry the non-working yarn along the edge of the pieces as you knit.

Decrease 1 stitch at the beginning and end of every 3 rows for 75 rows, or approximately 12½"/32 cm from cast-on edge—10 stitches total.

Work even for one row.

Increase 1 stitch at the beginning and end of every 3 rows for 39 rows, or approximately 18"/46 cm from cast-on edge—36 stitches total.

Work even for another 2"/5 cm and bind off after the second row of one of the color stripes.

LEFT TOP:

Cast on 36 stitches with yarn A. Like the Bottom, work the Left and Right Tops in stockinette stitch changing colors every 2 rows throughout to create the stripe pattern.

To make the drawstring casing, work even for 2"/5 cm, or 14 rows, ending with a wrong-side row.

At the armhole edge (the beginning of right-side rows), decrease 1 stitch every 3 rows for 42 rows. *At the same time,* at the center front edge, decrease 1 stitch at the end of every right-side row—2 stitches total. Bind off.

RIGHT TOP:

Cast on 36 stitches with yarn A. To make the drawstring casing, work even for 2"/5 cm, or 14 rows, ending with a wrong-side row.

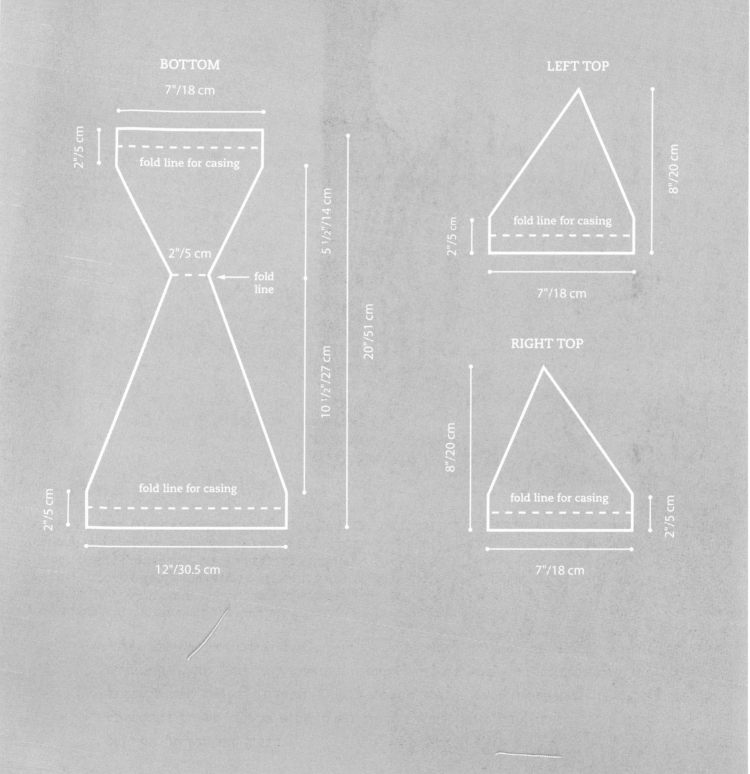

BOTTOM

7"/18 cm

2"/5 cm

fold line for casing

2"/5 cm

fold line

5 1/2"/14 cm

10 1/2"/27 cm

20"/51 cm

2"/5 cm

fold line for casing

12"/30.5 cm

LEFT TOP

8"/20 cm

2"/5 cm

fold line for casing

7"/18 cm

RIGHT TOP

8"/20 cm

fold line for casing

2"/5 cm

7"/18 cm

At the center front edge, decrease 1 stitch at the beginning of every right-side row starting with row 15. *At the same time,* at the armhole edge (the end of right-side rows), decrease 1 stitch every 3 rows for 42 rows—2 stitches total. Bind off.

FINISHING:
Weave in all loose ends with the tapestry needle.

With the crochet hook and yarn A, start at the center fold line of the Bottom (see diagram) and work single crochet around the entire piece.

With the crochet hook and yarn A, start at one of the corners on the bottom edge of the Left Top and work shell stitch around all the edges as follows:

Work 3 double crochet stitches into the same knit stitch, skip 3 stitches, slip stitch; repeat from * to * until you've worked around all edges. Work an extra shell stitch at any corners so the edging doesn't pull tightly.

Start at the same corner and repeat the same shell-stitch edging for the Right Top.

Fold over each of the drawstring casing edges 1"/2.5 cm from the edge and pin them down (see diagrams). You may find it helpful to iron each hem as well. Using the sewing needle and thread, hem the casings to the wrong side of the pieces. Make sure you leave openings at the sides.

With the crochet hook and two strands of yarn A, work two chains 42"/107 cm long and one chain 50"/127 cm long. Attach a wooden bead to the end of each chain by tying a small knot before and after each wooden bead. Thread one of the two 42"/107 cm chains through one of the casings of the Bottom piece and one through the other casing of the Bottom piece. Thread the 50"/127 cm chain through the casings on the Left and Right Top pieces.

To make the bikini top straps, use the crochet hook and two strands of yarn A to attach yarn at upper point of the Left Top (bind-off edge) and work a chain 21"/53 cm long. Repeat for the Right Top. Tie wooden beads to the end of each chain in the same way you did for the other straps.

With the crochet hook and 2 strands of yarn B, work a single chain 2½ yards/2.5 meters long. String 10 wooden beads on the chain and space them evenly (approximately 4"/10 cm apart) by tying knots in the chain before and after each bead. Use this chain to wrap around your bikini when you travel and as a great decorative belt when you're out getting some sun.

28. his and her vacation scarves

My grandfather used to wear a bicycle cap in his bicycle shop, which inspired the tweedy combination of these yarns. Both colors are unisex, so you can share. The thick cable running down the center is traditional but simple and fun to knit.

his and hers vacation scarves

Experience Level:
Intermediate

Size:
One size fits all

Finished Measurements:
7" wide × 60" long/18 cm × 152.5 cm

Yarn:
Hers Version:
A: 3 skeins Suss Cotton (100% cotton; 2.5 ounces/71 grams; 118 yards/109 meters),
color Honey
B: 3 skeins Suss Coolaid (85% acrylic/15% wool; 2 ounces/57 grams; 90 yards/83 meters),
color Natural
His Version:
A: 3 skeins Suss Cotton (100% cotton; 2.5 ounces/71 grams; 118 yards/109 meters),
color Willow
B: 3 skeins Suss Coolaid (85% acrylic/15% wool; 2 ounces/57 grams; 90 yards/83 meters),
color Olive

Notions:
- 1 pair size 13 (9 mm) needles
- 1 cable needle
  large tapestry needle
- 1 size H (5 mm) crochet hook

Gauge:
11 stitches and 13 rows = 4"/10 cm in cable pattern

SCARVES:
Cast on 20 stitches with one strand of yarn A and one strand of yarn B. Follow the 10-row cable pattern below until scarf measures approximately 60"/152.5 cm, ending with Row 10. Bind off in pattern.

CABLE PATTERN:
Rows 1 and 3: Knit 5 stitches, purl 2 stitches, knit 6, purl 2, knit 5.

Rows 2 and 4: Knit 7 stitches, purl 6, knit 7.

Row 5: Knit 5 stitches, purl 2, cable 6 forward (slip next 3 stitches onto cable needle *and place in front*, knit the next 3 stitches from the left-hand needle, and then knit the 3 stitches from the cable needle), purl 2, knit 5.

Rows 6, 8, and 10: Knit 7 stitches, purl 6, knit 7.

Rows 7 and 9: Knit 5 stitches, purl 2, knit 6, purl 2, knit 5.

FINISHING:
Weave in all loose ends with the tapestry needle.

To make the fringe, cut 40 lengths of both yarn A and yarn B approximately 14"/35.5 cm long each. Take 4 lengths of yarn A and 4 lengths of yarn B and fold them in half, forming a loop. Insert the crochet hook into one of the corners of the narrow edges of the scarf and pull the loop of yarn through from the other side of the scarf. Then pull the lengths of yarn through that loop and tighten to make your first fringe tassel. On each of the narrow edges of the scarf, make 5 fringe tassels placed about 1½"/4 cm apart.

60"/152.5 cm

7"/18 cm

29. all-season sweater

This is the perfect sweater for a honeymoon. I love the boatneck, which is almost off the shoulder. Knit in cuddly white yarn on big needles, it's got a beautiful, smooth finish. The bottom is reverse stockinette to give the sweater a bit of definition, while the natural shell buttons are elegant without being fussy. I predict you'll live in this sweater after the honeymoon because it's so versatile. Wear it over jeans for weekend getaways, with a gauzy skirt at the beach, or with white linen pants for strolling around shopping.

all-season sweater

Experience Level:
Intermediate

Sizes:
Small (medium, large, extra-large)

Finished Measurements:
Chest: 36" (38", 40", 42")/91 (96.5, 101.5, 106.5) cm
Length: 25" (26", 27", 28")/64 (66, 69, 71) cm

Yarn:
12 skeins Suss Snuggle (60% cotton/40% acrylic; 2 ounces/57 grams; 126 yards/
116 meters), color White

Notions:
- 1 pair size 11 (8 mm) needles
- 1 stitch holder
  large tapestry needle
  sewing pins
- 8 shell buttons, 1"/2.5 cm in diameter (available at www.sussdesign.com)

Gauge:
12 stitches and 17 rows = 4"/10 cm in stockinette stitch

SLEEVES:

Cast on 42 (44, 45, 46) stitches with two strands of yarn. Work in reverse stockinette stitch (purl all right-side rows and knit all wrong-side rows) for 16 rows.

Work in stockinette stitch (knit all right-side rows and purl all wrong-side rows) from this point forward. To make the switch from reverse stockinette to stockinette stitch, knit rows 16 *and* 17. Decrease 1 stitch at the beginning and end of every 16 (16, 16, 16) rows 3 times—36 (38, 39, 40) stitches, 64 (64, 64, 64) rows total.

Increase 1 stitch at the beginning and end of every 7 (8, 9, 9) rows 2 (2, 2, 2) times—40 (42, 43, 44) stitches, 78 (80, 82, 82) rows total.

To shape armholes, bind off 3 (3, 3, 3) stitches at the beginning of the next 2 rows—34 (36, 37, 38) stitches. Work even for 2 rows. Decrease 1 stitch at the beginning and end of every row for 10 rows. Bind off remaining 14 (16, 17, 18) stitches.

Make two.

BACK AND FRONT:

Cast on 54 (57, 60, 64) stitches with two strands of yarn. Work in reverse stockinette stitch for 16 rows.

Knit row 17 and work even in stockinette stitch until piece measures 17½" (18", 19", 20")/44.5 (46, 48.5, 51) cm, or approximately 74 (77, 81, 85) rows.

To shape armholes, bind off 3 stitches at the beginning of the next 2 rows—48 (51, 54, 58) stitches. Work even until piece measures 23½" (24½", 25½", 26½")/58.5 (62, 65, 67) cm, or approximately 100 (104, 108, 112) rows, ending with a wrong-side row.

Bind off 3 (3, 4, 3) stitches at the beginning of every row for 4 (4, 4, 6) rows. Bind off remaining 36 (39, 38, 40) stitches.

Make two.

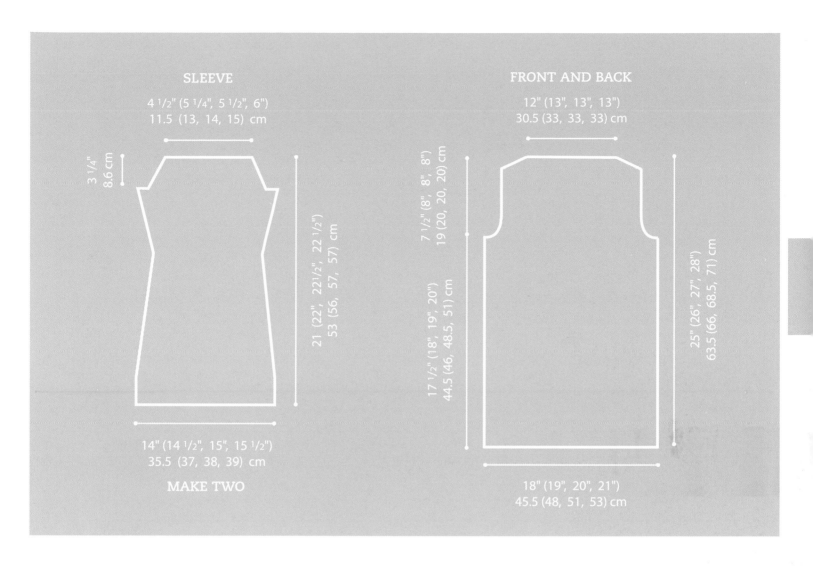

SLEEVE

4 ½" (5 ¼", 5 ½", 6")
11.5 (13, 14, 15) cm

3 ¼"
8.6 cm

21 (22", 22½", 22 ½")
53 (56, 57, 57) cm

14" (14 ½", 15", 15 ½")
35.5 (37, 38, 39) cm

MAKE TWO

FRONT AND BACK

12" (13", 13", 13")
30.5 (33, 33, 33) cm

7 ½" (8", 8", 8")
19 (20, 20, 20) cm

17 ½" (18", 19", 20")
44.5 (46, 48.5, 51) cm

25" (26", 27", 28")
63.5 (66, 68.5, 71) cm

18" (19", 20", 21")
45.5 (48, 51, 53) cm

FINISHING:

Weave in all loose ends with the tapestry needle.

Pin together the shoulder seams. With the tapestry needle and one strand of yarn, sew together the shoulder seams using backstitch.

Pin together and sew the side seams from the beginning of the armhole shaping to the reverse stockinette border. Leave the reverse stockinette border unseamed.

Pin together and sew the Sleeve seams leaving the reverse stockinette border unseamed. Pin the Sleeves into the armholes and sew the Sleeves to the body of the sweater using backstitch.

With the tapestry needle and one strand of yarn, attach four buttons total to the bottom edge of the sweater. One button should be sewn on approximately 1"/2.5 cm from each of the side seams on the line between the

reverse stockinette border and the stockinette stitch body of the sweater. Secure each button by wrapping the yarn a few times around the yarn shank of the button before tying off.

Repeat this process to attach two buttons to each of the sleeves on the line between the reverse stockinette stitch border and the stockinette stitch section.

Cut 4 lengths of yarn approximately 10"/25 cm long each. With the tapestry needle, attach 1 length to the underside of the sweater near one of the buttons. Insert the needle and thread through to the right side of the piece and wrap it around both buttons in a figure-eight pattern. Repeat for the other three pairs of buttons.

30. wraparound skirt

Throw this easygoing skirt in your suitcase and you'll be set for every occasion on your honeymoon. You decrease at different rates as you knit, which makes for a loose, flowing shape. The almost-shiny yarn contrasts with wooden beads that lend a little earthiness. Make it in several colors to mix and match with your favorite T-shirts and sweaters. It doesn't wrap as far around as traditional wrap skirts, so I recommend wearing it with a similarly colored top or over pants with high heels.

wraparound skirt

Experience Level:
Intermediate

Sizes:
Small (medium, large)

Finished Measurements:
Width: 48½" (50", 51 ½")/123.5 (127, 130.5) cm
Length: 22" (23", 24")/56 (58.5, 61) cm
Hip size: 36" (38", 40")/91.5 (96.5, 101.5) cm

Yarn:
8 skeins Suss Star (90% viscose/10% nylon; 1.5 ounces/43 grams; 126 yards/116 meters),
color Taupe

Notions:
1   pair size 5 (3.75 mm) circular needles, 24"/61 cm long
    size 5 (3.75 mm) double-pointed needles
1   knitting row counter
    large tapestry needle
    sewing pins (recommended)
1   size G (4 mm) crochet hook
6   wooden beads, 12 mm in diameter

Gauge:
24 stitches and 30 rows = 4"/10 cm in stockinette stitch

LEFT FRONT:

The Left Front and Right Front are worked with decreases on both edges that are worked at different rates. It is very important to keep track of the number of rows worked. When the right side (knit side) of the Left Front is facing you, the side seam will be the right edge and the center front edge will be the left edge.

Cast on 102 (105, 108) stitches. Work in stockinette stitch (knit all right-side rows and purl all wrong-side rows).

On the side seam (right) edge, decrease 1 stitch every 16 rows 10 (10, 11) times. Work even for 6 (12, 4) rows.

On the center front (left) edge, add 4 stitches every other row 4 times. Decrease 1 stitch every 16 rows 9 (10, 10) times. Work even for 14 (4, 12) rows.

Bind off.

RIGHT FRONT:

When the right side (knit side) of the Right Front is facing you, the side seam will be the left edge and the center front edge will be the right edge.

Cast on 96 (99, 102) stitches. Work in stockinette stitch.

On the side seam (left) edge, decrease 1 stitch every 13 (14, 15) rows 12 times. Work even for 10 (4, 0) rows at the same time.

On the center front (right) edge, add 4 stitches every other row 4 times. Decrease 1 stitch every 13 (13, 14) rows 12 times. Work even for 2 (8, 4) rows.

Bind off.

BACK PANEL:

Cast on 135 (138, 141) stitches. Work in stockinette

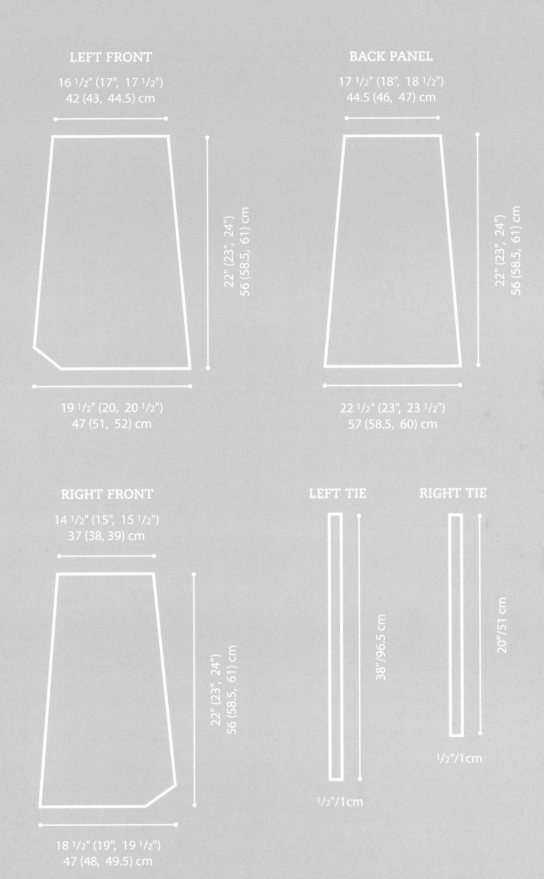

LEFT FRONT

16 ½" (17", 17 ½")
42 (43, 44.5) cm

22" (23", 24")
56 (58.5, 61) cm

19 ½" (20, 20 ½")
47 (51, 52) cm

BACK PANEL

17 ½" (18", 18 ½")
44.5 (46, 47) cm

22" (23", 24")
56 (58.5, 61) cm

22 ½" (23", 23 ½")
57 (58.5, 60) cm

RIGHT FRONT

14 ½" (15", 15 ½")
37 (38, 39) cm

22" (23", 24")
56 (58.5, 61) cm

18 ½" (19", 19 ½")
47 (48, 49.5) cm

LEFT TIE

38"/96.5 cm

½"/1cm

RIGHT TIE

20"/51 cm

½"/1cm

stitch, decreasing 1 stitch at the beginning and end of every 12 rows 8 (11, 15) times. For the largest size, bind off remaining 111 stitches. For the two smaller sizes, decrease 1 stitch at the beginning and end of every 10 rows 7 (4) times. Bind off remaining 105 (108) stitches.

Cast on 4 stitches with the double-pointed needles. Make an I-cord as follows:

Knit 4 stitches. With the right side facing you, slide these stitches from the left end of the double-pointed needle to the right end and switch this needle to your left hand. The right needle has now become the left needle. Bringing the working yarn around the back, knit the 4 stitches. Repeat until you have an I-cord that measures 20"/51 cm from the cast-on edge.

Bind off.

Cast on 4 stitches. Make an I-cord that measures 38"/96.5 cm from cast-on edge.

Bind off.

Weave in all loose ends with the tapestry needle.

Place the Left Front on top of the Back Panel with the right sides facing and sew the side seams together using backstitch. Keep the stitches very close to the edge to maintain the skirt's loose, flowing feel. You may find it helpful to pin all the pieces together before seaming.

Place the Right Front on top of the Back Panel with the right sides facing and sew the side seams using backstitch. Leave a ½"/1 cm opening approximately ½"/1 cm below the top edge (waist) for the tie to go through.

With the crochet hook and yarn, work a single crochet edging around the entire skirt.

With the tapestry needle and yarn, attach the Left Tie securely to the top edge (waist) corner of the Left Front. Attach the Right Tie to the top edge (waist) corner of the Right Front.

Thread 3 beads through the end of the Left Tie and tie a large knot. Repeat with the Right Tie.

Acknowledgments

This book, with its focus on weddings and marriage, family and friends, was wonderful—and fun—to make. I had a lot of help, as usual, from my own family and friends.

First, I'd like to thank all the models who made my designs look especially beautiful:

Hanna Cousins

Walter Driver

Ariana Gabisan

Josh Kritzer

Olia Lamar

Nadya Lateef

Gisela Marin

Grace Miller

Beth Orduna

Ashton Potts

Odessa Rae

Melanie Simons

Arielle Vandenberg and

Nichole Servin, who also helped with makeup.

Special thanks to:

Robin Glaser for makeup. I always love working with you.

Mandy Moneiro for hair.

Garrett Mastrogiovanni for being a florist with such incredible talent. A wedding needs flowers; they make everyone happy. Every picture grew out of your glorious arrangements.

Yoshie Shirai Eenigenburg for including me in her own beautiful wedding and, based on her experience, helping me style this book with extra enthusiasm and insight.

Kate Lonsdale, a wonderful person who once again helped me with pattern-making.

Everyone at Suss Design in the studio and at the store. I appreciate and adore you all. It has been many years of working together. And it takes team effort!

Evolutionary Media and Jennifer Gross. For helping me out with locations, especially the mansion where we shot the wedding, and for always being there.

Roosevelt Hotel for letting us shoot the honeymoon section in the Marilyn Monroe Suite.

Kum–Kum Sweden for the gorgeous jewelry.

Gisela Marin and Steven Werndorf for your beautiful house and for being my favorite friends.

Kaori Suzuki for your visionary photography and for making the book come to life—there are no words for such an incredible eye. It was a pleasure working with you and your partner and husband, Gene Shibuya. You both made it a breeze.

Karen Greenwald for technical editing.

Gretchen and Lee Twill and the whole Twill family for your very special tea and hospitality. Your Devi Tea calms me down and makes me feel there is another book on the horizon. I love you all.

Thanks Robin Dellabough and Lark Productions for yet another published book! Thanks for great work.

Potter Craft—this book was such a good project and let's hope it will help more people have beautiful weddings. You are all wonderful to work with.

Last, but never least, my own Brian, Hanna, and Viveka for loving me no matter what coast I happen to be on! I love you, my incredible family.

Yarn Substitution Guide

The following guide, organized by yarn weight, lists all the Suss yarns called for in this book and offers suggestions for substitution. As always, if you're not sure whether a particular yarn can be used as a substitute, try knitting a swatch first—does the gauge match? The fabric should also be similar in drape, texture, and appearance. The amount of yarn per skein varies, so be sure you base your substitution on the total yardage called for rather than the number of skeins.

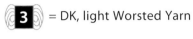 = DK, light Worsted Yarn

 = Worsted, Afghan, Aran yarn

 = DK, Bulky, Roving

LIGHT

Suss Angora: Any comparable weight angora or cashmere blend yarn

Suss Crisp: Any viscose yarn blended with a lightweight baby alpaca

Suss Fishnet: Any comparable lightweight alpaca blend

Suss Handpaint Mohair: Any comparable weight kidmohair silk blend

Suss Lurex: Any lightweight lurex blend yarn

Suss Meadow: Any light cotton with a light viscose

Suss Perle Cotton: Any fine, lightweight cotton yarn

Suss Silk: Any comparable weight silk

Suss Ultrasoft: Any comparable weight novelty viscose alpaca-nylon blend yarn

Suss Web: Any comparable weight baby alpaca–acrylic blend

MEDIUM

Suss Alpaca: Any comparable weight alpaca yarn

Suss Charm: Any medium-weight cotton plied with eyelash

Suss Cotton: Any comparable weight matte cotton yarn

Suss Crystal: Any comparable weight cotton and viscose blend

Suss Feather: Any polyamide fuzzy yarn of medium weight

Suss Icicle: Any comparable nylon blend with a sparkle look

Suss Melange: Any fine lightweight alpaca with fuzzy polyamide blend

Suss Snuggle: Any soft cotton or cotton-wool blend of comparable weight

Suss Star: Any medium-weight viscose blend

Suss Twisted: Any medium-weight slub cotton

BULKY

Suss Candy: Any bulky mohair-rayon-polyester novelty blend yarn with lash effect

Suss Coolaid: Any bulky wool yarn with slub texture

Resources

Suss yarn is available at Suss Design located at 7350 Beverly Boulevard, Los Angeles, California 90036 (telephone: 323-954-9637). The store stocks a complete line of yarns from all the best manufacturers and Suss brand yarns. Shoppers can also find needles, patterns, and a complete collection of notions (buttons, beads, crochet and leather decorations) needed for projects in Suss's books. Specialty items include Suss's hand cream for knitters, and a customized blend of tea.

Knitters around the country can purchase Suss yarns as well as many of the notions featured in this book at the Suss Design website, www.sussdesign.com.

STORES THAT CARRY SUSS YARN:

Alaska
Yarn Branch of The Quilt Tree
341 E. Benson Blvd. #5
Anchorage, AK 99503
907-561-4115
www.quiltree.com

California
Article Pract
5010 Telegraph Ave.
Oakland, CA 94609
510-595-7875
www.articlepract.com

Devrie Christina's Knittery
1202 Grant Ave. Suite A1
Novato, CA 94945
415-236-1536

Three Dog Knit
475 N. Lake Blvd. Suite 103
Tahoe City, CA 96145
530-583-0001
www.threedogknit.com

Connecticut
Knitting Central
582 Post Rd. East
Westport, CT 06880
203-454-4300
www.knittingcentral.com

Illinois
Chix with Stix
7316 W. Madison St.
Forest Park, IL 60130
708-366-6300
www.chixwithstixknitting.com

Loopy Yarns
719 South State St.
Chicago, IL 60605
312-583-9276
www.loopyyarns.com

Minnesota
Digs
310 Division St. South
Northfield, MN 55057
507-664-9140
www.shopdigs.com

New York
Wild Wools
732 South Ave.
Rochester, NY 14620
585-271-0960
www.wildwoolsyarn.com

Oklahoma
Loops
2042 Utica Square
Tulsa, OK 74114
918-742-9276
www.loopsknitting.com

Pennsylvania
Loop
1914 South St.
Philadelphia, PA 19146
215-893-9939
www.loopyarn.com

Canada
Room 6
4389 Gallant Ave.
Deep Cove, N. Vancouver
British Columbia
V7G 1L1
604-628-8484
www.room6.com

NOTIONS:

A.C. Moore Arts & Crafts
www.acmoore.com

Auntie's Beads
866-262-3237
www.auntiesbeads.com

Beadworks
800-232-3761
www.beadworks.com/us/

CraftA.com
888-327-2382
www.crafta.com

Flax
888.352.9278
www.flaxart.com

Hobby Lobby
800-888-0321
www.hobylobby.com

JewelrySupply
866-380-7464
www.jewelrysupply.com

Jo-Ann Fabric & Crafts
www.joann.com

Kate's Paperie
800.809.9880
www.katespaperie.com

Michael's
800-642-4235
www.michaels.com

Pearl Paints
800-451-7327
www.pearlpaint.com

About the Author

SUSS COUSINS, the author of three previous knitting books, grew up in Sweden where her

grandmother taught her to knit and where, at the age of 19, she opened her first boutique. After moving to New York in 1982, she tended bar by night and knit sweaters by day. ✳ Since coming to the U.S., she has grown her business from designing custom pieces for a small roster of loyal clients to designing complete lines of fashion knitwear for men, women and children. Her inspired designs are available at her retail store in Los Angeles, as well as at boutiques and department stores throughout the country, including Bergdorf Goodman, Barney's, and Neiman Marcus. ✳ Suss also designs for television and film. Suss's unique knit costumes have been featured in movies such as *Last Holiday, Underdog, Cat in the Hat, Shall We Dance, The Matrix, Master and Commander, Men in Black,* and *How the Grinch Stole Christmas* and on TV shows like *The OC, Gilmore Girls, Curb Your Enthusiasm, Will and Grace,* and *Friends.* ✳ Knitters clamor for her yarns and patterns and flock to her website (www.sussdesign.com) and her popular classes. Suss has produced an instructional DVD on knitting called "Learn to Knit." ✳ Suss lives in Los Angeles with her husband and two daughters.

Index